Back to Basics

Back to Basics
Ethics for Behavior Analysts

Amanda N. Kelly, PhD, BCBA-D, LBA
Behaviorbabe

Emily Shraga, MA, BCBA
Behavior Specialist, Fredericksburg City
Public Schools

Lara Bollinger, JD, BCBA
Attorney, Shub & Associates, P.C.

ELSEVIER

Academic Press is an imprint of Elsevier
125 London Wall, London EC2Y 5AS, United Kingdom
525 B Street, Suite 1650, San Diego, CA 92101, United States
50 Hampshire Street, 5th Floor, Cambridge, MA 02139, United States
The Boulevard, Langford Lane, Kidlington, Oxford OX5 1GB, United Kingdom

Back to Basics: Ethics for Behavior Analysts

Notices
Knowledge and best practice in this field are constantly changing. As new research and experience broaden our understanding, changes in research methods, professional practices, or medical treatment may become necessary.

Practitioners and researchers must always rely on their own experience and knowledge in evaluating and using any information, methods, compounds, or experiments described herein. In using such information or methods they should be mindful of their own safety and the safety of others, including parties for whom they have a professional responsibility.

To the fullest extent of the law, neither nor the Publisher, nor the authors, contributors, or editors, assume any liability for any injury and/or damage to persons or property as a matter of products liability, negligence or otherwise, or from any use or operation of any methods, products, instructions, or ideas contained in the material herein.

ISBN: 978-0-323-85566-2

For information on all Academic Press publications visit our website at
https://www.elsevier.com/books-and-journals

Publisher: Nikki P. Levy
Senior Acquisitions Editor: Joslyn T. Chaiprasert-Paguio
Editorial Project Manager: Tracy I. Tufaga
Publishing Services Manager: Shereen Jameel
Project Manager: Vishnu T. Jiji
Senior Designer: Vicky Pearson Esser

Working together
to grow libraries in
developing countries

www.elsevier.com • www.bookaid.org

Last digit is the print number: 9 8 7 6 5 4 3 2 1

Contents

SECTION 5: Responsibility in public statements 91

SECTION 6: Responsibility in research 105

Dedication

We dedicate this book to Feda and
Muhammed Almaliti, fierce autism
advocates who dedicated—and sacrificed
their lives. In our actions, may their
memories live on.

Acknowledgments

We would like to acknowledge Drs. Linda LeBlanc, Thomas Freeman, and Jose Martinez-Diaz, as well as Drs. Nancy Rosenberg and Eileen Schwartz for their ethical decision-making frameworks, which we reference often throughout this text.

Teaching ancillaries for this book, including Essay Questions and Multiple-Choice Questions, are available online to qualified instructors. Visit https://educate.elsevier.com/book/details/9780323855662 for more information and to register for access.

Introduction and roadmap for ethical decision making

"What you do makes a difference, and you have to decide what kind of difference you want to make."

Jane Goodall

Originally a topic of discussion for religious scholars and philosophers, ethics is now the focus for various disciplines, including the field of behavior analysis. Developing a code of ethics, morals, and values aids communities in determining what is right and what is wrong. Codes of conduct are not specific to behavior analysts; they also exist in other professions, such as medicine, law, journalism, and accounting. When discussing ethics, we are generally referring to an investigation of moral principles and dilemmas.

Behavioral ethics is the study of why people make the decisions they do. Not unlike behavior analysis, behavioral ethics focuses on observable and measurable behaviors, rather than theoretical or hypothetical abstractions. Behavioral ethics, and likely our own personal experiences, have taught us

Back to Basics. https://doi.org/10.1016/B978-0-323-85566-2.00001-8

1

that the decisions we make are far from rational. Oftentimes, we make decisions from a place of emotion, rather than after a careful and calculated analysis.

Ethical dilemmas are difficult to navigate, requiring analytical thinking, as ethics is hardly ever black or white. When navigating ethical dilemmas, often there is no exact right or wrong answer, which is what makes ethical challenges so challenging. To determine if something is ethical or unethical, we must ask ourselves a series of questions. While science is objective and based on quantifiable data, sometimes the answer we are seeking is simpler to achieve. Before creating tools and checklists and charts and fancy matrices, we recommend beginning with a simple gut check. After all, being parsimonious is also a tenet of scientific inquiry.

We intentionally chose a spider web for the cover of this book. When we authors think of ethics, we think of intricate and complex scenarios, much like the web of a spider. Ethics can be tricky and sticky to navigate, and oftentimes, just like the silky strings of a web, ethical dilemmas become more or less translucent, depending on the angle of the light. As noted by poet Paul Eldridge (1966), "In the spider-web of facts, many a truth is strangled."

Throughout this text, you will find questions and suggestions for how to navigate difficult situations. We hope to simplify and demystify the often-complicated discussions surrounding ethics and making ethical decisions. Throughout this text, we have created questions and scenarios for you to ponder and discuss, while providing tools, readings, research, and resources to help you along the way. We begin the book with this roadmap, providing an overview of ethics and ethical decision making. Following this chapter, you will see that each of the next six chapters aligns with the corresponding section of the Behavior Analyst Certification Board's (BACB) Ethics Code for Behavior Analysts. We begin each chapter by listing the relevant ethics code standards and posing three guiding questions. Our goal is to orient our readers to the salient components of each ethics code section. Throughout each chapter, we include scenarios for you to ponder and then discuss with peers or partners. At the end of each chapter, we incorporate a list of additional discussion questions for you to deliberate, debate, and discuss. We also encourage you to continue your inquiry well beyond the pages of this book. In addition to discussion questions, we embed related readings and podcast episodes, which we list at the end of each chapter. Our hope is that you will immerse yourself in the literature and resources available. Whenever you find yourself feeling overwhelmed or uncertain, we hope you will recall the guidance from the authors of this text, as well as the advice, recommendations, and suggestions that come from this robust community of seasoned experts in our field through the ancillary resources we provide.

Roadmap for ethical decision making

When presented with a potential ethical conundrum, Freeman, LeBlanc, & Martinez-Diaz (2020) implore us to explore three important questions: "1) What is the right thing to do? 2) What is worth doing? and 3) What does it mean to be a good behavior analyst?".

Imagine the following scenario: A school district asks you to complete an assessment for a student. You ask to see the signed consent for assessment from the caregiver. The administrator tells you "The caregivers consented, believe me," but the third party is unable to produce a copy of the written consent. Let us begin by asking ourselves "What is the right thing to do?" In this case, you are being asked to conduct an assessment without any documentation that the client or the client's legal guardian has consented to the evaluation. The potential of harm to the client is significant, as you do not have permission to review records, interview others, or interface with the client or the client's caregiver. Next we ask "What is worth doing?" As behavior analysts, we also do not provide services to anyone who has not consented and contracted us to do so. We may seek to obtain consents, or we may inform our employer that we cannot conduct the assessment until we do. Moving to the third question, "What does it mean to be a good behavior analyst," we determine that a "good" behavior analyst is someone who is honest and truthful while acting with integrity and in "the best interest of their clients" (BACB, 2020, 1.03). Asking ourselves these questions leads us to determine that the right thing to do is to decline to conduct this assessment, unless the school obtains proper consent.

In some situations, these questions may leave us unsure of what to do. Rosenberg and Schwartz (2019), authors of "Guidance or Compliance," present a six-step decision-making process. These six steps are (1) identifying if there is an ethical concern, (2) brainstorming solutions, (3) evaluating solutions, (4) determining if there is a solution/clear course of action, (5) implementing the solution with fidelity and integrity, and (6) reflecting on our results.

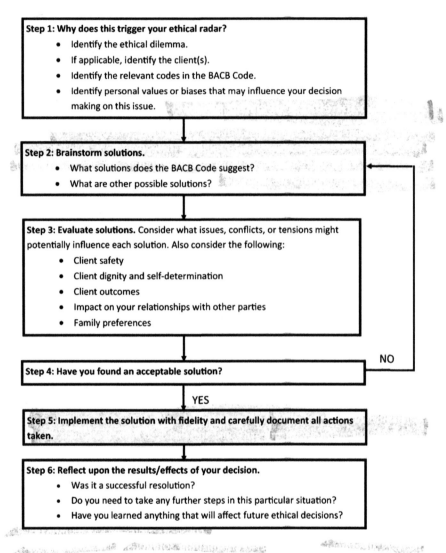

The first step of identifying if an ethical concern exists may seem simple; however, it is a valid place to begin. There are times when something may not feel right or is not congruent with our own beliefs or values, but our professional standards may not consider it unethical. In these cases, we may not need to continue with the remaining steps in the process, as an ethical concern does not exist. On the other hand, if we identify a need for further inquiry, Rosenberg and Schwartz (2019) suggest brainstorming solutions, which begin by walking through the Professional and Ethical Compliance Code for Behavior Analysts (PECC; BACB, 2014), which has now been updated to the Ethics Code for Behavior Analysts (BACB, 2020). You may also wish to brainstorm solutions by reaching out to mentors and professors and reviewing the literature, while keeping in mind the relevant sections of our ethics code. You are not likely to find a prescriptive ("Do this") answer; however you will have a handful of ideas to consider when determining what to do next. After brainstorming ideas, Rosenberg and Schwartz instruct us to evaluate these ideas and to identify possible solutions. This process may include creating a pros and cons list, or what we often refer to as a risk-benefit analysis. Once we have evaluated our options, we must determine if there is a clear course of action. If there is, we should move forward with what we have determined is the best next step. If we are still unsure of what we should do, Rosenberg and Schwartz suggest we return to brainstorming ideas, perhaps reaching out to the authors of related research publications or other experts in the field. After we determine which course of action to take, we must create systems and conditions that allow us to carry out these actions with fidelity and integrity. "Thus, it is critically important that a behavior analyst documents the steps taken both in arriving at a decision and in carrying out the decision" (Rosenberg & Schwartz, p. 479). This process may look like creating a checklist for supervisees to use when performing an assessment or creating a fidelity checklist for technicians to use when implementing a behavior plan. Lastly, we must reflect on the outcomes and the results of our decisions. Did we protect the client? Did we advocate for the best interest of the client with all stakeholders? How did we document our advocacy efforts and the recommendations we provided? What can we learn from this experience to inform future situations?

Let us look at another scenario and use this six-step process to identify a solution or next course of action for the client: A dear friend has a son who has recently been diagnosed with autism and has received a recommendation for applied behavior analysis (ABA) services. However, there are no providers in the area. Your friend asks if she can pay you privately to consult with her and provide direct services to her son. In this situation, the potential for harm if the child goes without services could be quite high. However, the potential for harm that can occur from dual relationships may present a conflict of interest and can also be significant. A "good" behavior analyst is one who is compassionate and helpful, as well as objective and professional. So, what is the right thing to do? Let us explore this scenario using the six-step ethical decision-making process of Rosenberg and Schwartz (2019):

1. Identify and name the concern
   a. Gut check: What is the potential for harm?
   b. Ethical walkthrough: Select two or three applicable codes. Without support, this child in need of ABA services may not access care. This dual relationship between the analyst and the caregiver (e.g., friendship) may also present a conflict of interest.
2. Brainstorm solutions
   a. Source of information: BACB Code, publications, mentors, experts.
   b. Salient points to consider: Dual relationships may present a conflict of interest, which may impact our ability to be objective and honest with the client. This conflict of interest could impact fidelity and adherence to treatment protocols. If behaviors intensify or if a disagreement ensues, it will also damage the friendship.

3. Evaluate solutions
   a. What does it mean to be a "good" behavior analyst? A "good" behavior analyst would do everything possible to help a friend's child access care. A good behavior analyst would understand the value of objective evaluation and the risk of harm associated with multiple relationships.
   b. What is the right thing to do? The right thing to do would be to make a referral to another provider, including consideration of remote options. You may also compile resources and provide information on obtaining support.
4. Make a determination
   a. Prioritize the client/vulnerable individual.
   b. Document conversations and decisions. Using this decision-making rubric is one way to document your thoughts and actions throughout this process
   c. Decision: More to consider? Decision made? When the decision is made to refer to another provider, compile resources (e.g., books, support groups, etc.) to share with your friend.
5. Implement with fidelity and integrity
   a. Document conversations and decisions.
   b. Inform all stakeholders. Be kind, compassionate, and clear. Tell your friend that you are not ethically (and in many cases legally) able to provide services to anyone with whom you already have an existing relationship. This news may likely hurt or disappoint your friend. Prepare yourself for this reaction. When your friend is ready or able, offer to make referrals and provide additional information and resources that may be helpful, including for their child.
6. Reflect upon results
   a. How did I ensure protections for the vulnerable individual? Although you may have been able to help this child "enter into care" sooner if you had accepted this individual as a client, you would have created conditions that would lead to future threats of harm. The decision is a difficult one to make, but in the long run the benefits of your decision outweigh the risks to which you may have exposed the child.
   b. How effectively did I communicate the decision with all stakeholders? Was I prepared for a negative reaction? Did my actions damage my personal relationship?
   c. How effectively did I document my advocacy and recommendations? Did I reach out to others? If so, did I keep copies of emails exchanged? Did I write down the date and times of phone calls and what was discussed?
   d. What can I learn from this experience to inform future situations? Would it be helpful to have a script of what to say in the future if a friend announces that their child has an autism diagnosis? For example: *"I know there's a lot of overwhelming information out there. I am happy to connect you with other experts and information to help your child access services."*

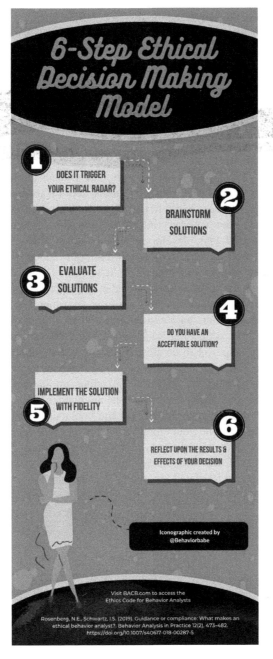

FIGURE I.2   Infographic containing a visual flow chart of the six-step decision-making model from "Guidance or Compliance" by Rosenberg and Schwartz (2019).

Behaving ethically can be hard to do, especially when there is no handbook with prescriptive answers of what we should do in each scenario. It can be painful, even heartbreaking, to turn away a friend or to decline to conduct an assessment. Since what we want to do is operate in the best interest of the client, it can be easy to rationalize how conducting that assessment may help the client eventually access services. Although that may be true in the immediate sense, we must also consider the long-term impacts of our decisions. Using a worksheet such as the one provided in this book will help us make thoughtful and objective decisions when it comes to us navigating complex and sticky ethical situations.

The BACB also provides an 11-step ethical decision-making process within the Ethics Code. This resource is another tool for us to use when facing ethical dilemmas. It does not lead to the "right" answer, but the steps provide a guide for gathering the necessary information, examining your own learning history, and potential bias, developing various courses of action, and challenging you to select the course of action that both reduces risk to the client and resolves the ethical dilemma. The BACB's 11-step decision-making process highlights the need to seek out other resources when examining the situation. These other resources can come from your mentors, reaching out to researchers or practitioners with expertise in that area, or even contacting the ABA Ethics Hotline, which Jon Bailey and several colleagues run. This hotline, in turn, can help you to create a community that supports you in your practice but also elevates the practice of ethical behavior analysis. The BACB also provides a plethora of resources on ethics on its website, including toolkits, ethics-related newsletters, podcasts, an interactive historical timeline, and a list of ethics-related journal articles and books dating back to 2003. An additional resource can be your state's behavior analysis association. In fact, the Arizona Association for Behavior Analysis provides an Ethics Scenario Archive consisting of over 40 scenarios that are accessible to the public. There is no shortage of ethics-related resources. You do not have to walk through your ethical dilemma on your own.

11-Step Ethical Decision - Making BACB Process	
1	Clearly define the issue and consider potential risk of harm to relevant individuals.
2	Identify all relevant individuals.
3	Gather relevant supporting documentation and follow -up on second hand information to confirm that there is an actual ethical concern.
4	Consider your personal learning history and biases in the context of the relevant individuals.
5	Identify the relevant core principles and code standards.
6	Consult available resources (e.g., research, decision-making models, trusted colleagues).
7	Develop several possible actions to reduce or remove risk of harm, prioritizing the best interests of clients in accordance with the code and applicable laws.
8	Critically evaluate each possible action by considering its alignment with the "letter and spirit" of the code, its potential impact on the client and stakeholders, the likelihood of it immediately resolving the ethical concern, and variables such as client preference, social acceptability, degree of restrictiveness, and likelihood of maintenance.
9	Select the action that seems most likely to resolve the specific ethical concern and reduce the likelihood of similar issues arising in the future.
10	Take the selected action in collaboration with relevant individuals affected by the issue and document specific actions taken, agreed-upon next steps, names of relevant individuals, and due dates.
11	Evaluate the outcomes to ensure that the action successfully addressed the issue.

Behavior Analyst Certification Board. (2020). Ethics code for behavior analysts.
https://bacb.com/wp-content/ethics-code-for-behavior-analysts

FIGURE I.3   Chart listing the 11-step decision-making model by the BACB (2020).

Core principles

In the most recent edition of the BACB Ethics Code, the introduction includes information about the scope and application of the code, its core principles, and considerations for ethical decision making. The document describes these core principles as "foundational principles, which all behavior analysts should strive to embody" (BACB, 2020, p. 4). The Ethics Code instructs us to use these principles to "interpret and apply" each ethical code standard (BACB). The four core principles outlined in the BACB Ethics Code include a commitment to (1) benefit others, (2) treat others with compassion, dignity, and respect, (3) behave with integrity, and (4) ensure competence.

FIGURE I.4 Infographic containing the four core principles outlined in the BACB Ethics Code (2020).

Benefit others

As behavior analysts, we must operate in the best interest of our clients. We work to maximize benefits and to do no harm by "protecting the welfare of our clients above all others" (BACB, 2020, p. 4). In addition, we must operate in the best interest of our trainees and supervisees, as well as all individuals with whom we interact in a professional capacity. This step means that as analysts we are focusing on and evaluating both the short-term and long-term effects of our professional interactions. An article published in an early behavior analytic journal that embodies much of the same sentiment is "Social Validity: The Case for Subjective Measurement or How Behavior Analysis Is Finding Its Heart" by Montrose Wolf (1978). In this article, Wolf urges us to consider the acceptability of our treatments and procedures from the point of view of our consumers, in addition to the objective outcomes we often use to measure success. Wolf makes a case for us to blend social validity, a subjective impression of our effectiveness, with data and other objective measures. Let us, as analysts, find our hearts, connect with our colleagues and clients, and use the data we collect to paint a picture, thus enabling us to tell a more complete, compassionate account of the science of behavior change. Two decades later, Carr and colleagues (1999) generated a publication entitled "An Assessment of Social Validity Trends in Applied Behavior Analysis." This article reviews all studies published on social validity measures in the *Journal of Applied Behavior Analysis* within the first three decades of the publication's history. The authors found that most of the studies reviewed did not include measures of social validity. Of the studies that did, interventions provided in more natural environments were found to be rated with higher social validity. We have an ethical obligation to design and deliver effective treatment, which involves clients and stakeholders—meaning that there must be an assessment of the social validity of targets identified, interventions selected, and outcomes achieved. This article highlights the need for published interventions to include such measures in our analysis.

Behaving for the benefit of others also means determining and resolving the potential impact our own physical and mental health has on our ability to be effective as behavior analysts (BACB, 2020). In a 2020 podcast episode, Jackie MacDonald discusses balance, being present, and pausing our fast-paced brains. MacDonald poses the question of how often "overachievers" in the helping professions stop to check in and take care of ourselves (Kelly, 2020b). In this episode, listeners will find a fun and lighthearted conversation about creating balance and hear how MacDonald is learning to reinforce her own "hobbyist" behaviors. These examples can help you identify and address your own physical and mental health needs by reminding you of the necessary step of checking in with yourself. Just as we are given the instruction to put on our own oxygen mask on an airplane before assisting others, as members of the helping profession we need to ensure that we are physically and mentally healthy enough to assist our clients.

A commitment to benefiting others also includes a responsibility to identify potential conflicts of interest and to create plans and systems to resolve these conflicts. As behavior analysts, we commit to "effectively and respectfully collaborating with others in the best interest of our clients" (BACB, 2020, p. 4). It is equally important for us as behavior analysts to identify and address factors (e.g., financial, personal, institutional, etc.) that might lead to conflicts of interest or abuse of one's position. We never want to put our clients, supervisees, or colleagues in situations where they feel pressure to agree with our recommendations or directives, which is more likely to occur when multiple relationships exist. Behavior analysts must be careful to protect the trust our clients, and relevant stakeholders, place in us.

Treat others with compassion, dignity, and respect

In addition to working to benefit others, as behavior analysts we have a commitment to treating all individuals equitably, regardless of factors such as age, disability, ethnicity, gender expression, or any other basis prescribed by law. As outlined in our ethics code, behavior analysts have a commitment to respect and promote our clients' self-determination to the best of our ability, particularly when providing services to vulnerable populations. There is significant value in listening to the communities we serve and learning their perspectives as recipients of behavior analytic services. Involving clients in their programming has been a tenet of behavior analytic practice for decades. However, the degree to which we seek to do this as a community continues to evolve and increase in recent years. In several cases, these insights have led to programmatic and procedural shifts in teaching protocols. For example, several autistic individuals have described that making eye contact is painful, and programming focusing on increasing eye contact may be causing significant distress, particularly for individuals on the autism spectrum. As a result of this information, many behavior analytic communication programs and language protocols have shifted to other ways of indicating engagement, such as by orienting toward the speaker, or being in close proximity to discussion partners. We invite our readers to learn directly from self-advocates about their experiences on the autism spectrum, as well as from others who love and care for them.

In recent years, there has been an increase in hurtful and hateful discourse within the autism community, particularly toward caregivers who advocate on behalf of ABA. In a 2021 podcast episode (Kelly, 2021), Eileen Lamb—author, photographer, artist, and mom—speaks about her family's relationship with autism. Lamb shares her journey to receiving an autism diagnosis, as well as what it is like being a mom to two boys on the autism spectrum. Lamb describes for listeners the good, the bad, and the ugly— detailing the cyberbullying attacks she has been a victim of when publicly promoting ABA for her children. In addition, Lamb details some of the horrific comments that have been made and shares how she has learned to navigate the negativity, creating a safe space on social media platforms for caregivers and community members who wish to engage in meaningful and respectful dialogue.

Another example of the evolution of ABA practices toward a more compassionate approach involves an investigation of the televisability of particular procedures (Hanley, 2021). In some cases, behavior technicians, teachers, and caregivers have been encouraged to "remove attention" or "remain neutral" when a child or client is upset or in distress. We may have been taught that providing attention will intensify or reinforce the behavior, and therefore we have been instructed—or have instructed others—to withdraw attention and engage in "planned ignoring." When we think about the acceptability of such procedures, we should question whether the protocols we are following and the procedures we are implementing can easily be described as kind, compassionate, humane, and televisable (Hanley, 2021). Simply because we were taught one way does not mean we should indefinitely practice that way for the entirety of our careers. We must grow and adapt and commit to continually evolving our approach in the best interest of the clients we serve. As poignantly stated by Jonathan Tarbox, "[W]e have to be human beings first, we have to respect human dignity and compassion first. And if we're not sure if we're doing a good enough job of that or not, that's where we stop. Put the brakes on. Say, 'Hang on a second. We need to reassess this.' We are not just going to accept something if we have serious concerns about whether it is ethical or moral" (El Fattal, 2022).

Many individuals in the provider community also have concerns about particular practices and experiences in the field. In Harrison 2019, Antonio Harrison raised concerns within the profession, pertaining to areas such as lack of diversity and discriminatory behavior witnessed toward particular subgroups. Harrison candidly admits he contemplated "divorcing" the field and abandoning the science. In the 2020 podcast episode "Turning On the Lights" (Kelly, 2020a), Harrison discusses his open letter to the field of behavior analysis, detailing concerns with lack of representation in our field, and his overall feeling of disappointment and exhaustion. In the conversation, he elaborates on these sentiments, while also presenting hope and providing ideas on how we can effectively evolve and expand our reach as behavior scientists.

In a subsequent podcast (Kelly, 2020d), Julia Fiebig describes her journey as a behavior analyst, classical violinist, songwriter, and climate change activist. Fiebig discusses the value for analysts to fluently learn the science of behavior analysis. In this episode, she shares the growth we can achieve when we are willing to place ourselves in uncomfortable situations—whether that is attending a conference where you are the only behavior analyst or presenting to a room full of others outside of our profession. It can be daunting and difficult but, as Fiebig shows us, totally doable, too.

Many individuals have weighed in on concerns and threats to our field throughout the years, and we find the most attractive discussions to be those that focus on utilizing our science to identify solutions and actuate change. An article authored by Bridget Taylor, Linda LeBlanc, and Melissa Nosik titled "Compassionate Care in Behavior Analytic Treatment: Can Outcomes Be Enhanced by Attending to Relationships with Caregivers?" explores ways in which behavior analysts can develop "fluency in relationship-building skills that strengthen the commitment to treatment" (2018, p. 654). The authors are seasoned analysts who have seen the significant growth and growing pains associated with the expansion of our field. In this paper, they detail the needs of our field as well as strategies for cultivating and enhancing relationship-building skills.

Behavioral scientist E. Scott Geller also discusses the importance of compassion, embodying this sentiment through his teachings on actively caring for others. Geller discusses this approach again in a podcast (Kelly, 2019) and advocates for more effective dissemination of compassion in our science. He engages listeners with stories of daily, real-life applications from his personal experiences and shares outcomes related to taking an actively caring approach to all that we do.

Behave with integrity

Behavior analysts work with various populations, often with individuals who are some of the most vulnerable in our society (e.g., Individuals with Developmental Disability (IDD), Autism Spectrum Disorder (ASD), ODD (Oppositional Defiant Disorder)). To ensure that the interests of our clients are protected and kept at the heart of what we do as behavior analysts, we agree to behave in an honest and trustworthy manner, to avoid misrepresenting our work or others' work, and to follow through on obligations, ensuring we are meeting responsibilities and keeping our promises. To behave with integrity also includes holding ourselves accountable for our work and for the work of those we supervise. To behave with integrity, behavior analysts must be knowledgeable about regulatory requirements and aim to uphold these expectations as we work to create professional and ethical environments. For many of us, our awareness must extend to include state licensure requirements. Given the rise in remote, telehealth, and telemedicine services, due in large part to the COVID-19 pandemic, it has become increasingly important for behavior analysts to know the laws and regulations not only for states where they live but also for each state where they practice. To access current information on the status of licensure initiatives in the United States, we refer readers to the resources found via the Association of Professional Behavior Analysts (APBA).

Ensure competence

As behavior analysts, when accepting clients we have the expectation to ensure our own competence by practicing within the parameters of the science.

The expectation is that we are not only aware of what lies within the profession's scope of practice, but also that we are aware of our individual scope of competence, based on our own history, education, and training. To become certified in behavior analysis, one must undergo rigorous training, coursework, and supervision requirements, in addition to passing national board examinations. We should recognize and applaud the elevation of these standards, yet they are the requirements for meeting only the minimum standards to practice. That is why the BACB requires ongoing engagement in continuing education activities for behavior analysts, which may include attending and presenting at conferences, as well as reviewing and contributing to research and/or the peer review process. We must establish and ensure our competence by remaining knowledgeable about current trends—and not only scientific advancement but also pseudoscientific or fad claims. By remaining engaged and immersed with current trends, we are in a better position to educate stakeholders and inform our clients of the potential risks and benefits associated with each option.

Part of developing and extending our competence involves continually increasing our knowledge and skills related to cultural responsiveness and their influence on effective service delivery. These considerations are particularly important, as behavior analysts are likely to serve a diverse group of learners from various cultures and backgrounds. Patricia Wright frequently leads discussions centered on cultural humility in our field. In her presentations and publications, Wright describes how we classify culture as our social habits, religion, language, and beyond. She discusses the difference between cultural competence and cultural humility, sharing that *competence* presumes the achievement of a final goal or outcome, whereas *humility* lends itself to being an ongoing endeavor. For behavior analysts, being culturally aware includes adapting our language, especially when we are working with other professions or cultures. We strongly suggest reading her 2019 publication titled "Cultural Humility in the Practice of Applied Behavior Analysis," as well as listening to the podcast episode where Wright shares some of her own missteps and lessons learned, modeling for us all how we can work toward becoming more humble humans (Kelly, 2020e).

Justin Leaf is a researcher who presents a progressive approach to applied behavior analysis. In a podcast episode titled "Ensuring a Bright Future for our Field," Leaf discusses concerns in the field of behavior analysis and offers suggestions for how we can propel our practices forward (Kelly, 2020c). Leaf reminds us to select socially significant treatment targets and to be flexible when implementing treatment protocols. Leaf also encourages us to be okay being uncomfortable, to remain open-minded, and to be willing to engage in professional discourse with one another.

In "What counts as high-quality practitioner training in applied behavior analysis?" (Critchfield, 2015), the author investigates for ABA practitioners the role of research training, exploring what universities and faculty can do to establish a strong, research-driven examination of variables that frequently arise in practice. Simply because someone has been trained, or because a program offers training, does not mean the training will be sufficient to produce high-quality outcomes or competence in the practitioner. This article explores actionable steps supervisors can take, and supervisees can demand, to produce meaningful outcomes.

Before we can dive directly into the BACB Ethics Code, we would be remiss not to take a quick look at the history of ethics as it pertains to our field. Figure I.5 provides a historical timeline of the evolution of ethics from the BACB. The BACB was established in 1998 and introduced, in 1999, the first iteration of our ethics code, which was called the Professional Disciplinary Standards. This document gave the BACB power to issue sanctions to certificants in limited circumstances. As we can see from Figure I.5, our ethics code has been revised many times as new situations have arisen, our field has grown, and new technology has required additional protections for consumers of our services. In addition, ethics coursework was not initially required as part of the BACB's requirements. In 2002, the BACB recognized the importance of ethics and began requiring 15 credit hours of ethics coursework for all BCBA applicants, expanding this requirement to 45 credit hours in 2015. In 2007, the BACB added a requirement for continuing education in ethics, recognizing the need to stay current in the ever-evolving web of ethical dilemmas faced by analysts.

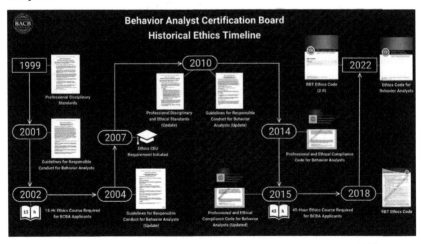

FIGURE I.5 BACB Ethics Timeline displaying the changes to the ethics code from 1999 to 2022.

Throughout the other sections of this book, we revisit the BACB's core principles and ethical decision-making models by incorporating them further into our discussions. Although no text can explore every scenario or question, our goal is to provide you, our readers, with a robust set of resources that we hope will prove useful for navigating ethical dilemmas you may encounter.

References

Carr, J. E., Austin, J. L., Britton, L. N., Kellum, K. K., & Bailey, J. S. (1999). An assessment of social validity trends in applied behavior analysis. *Behavioral Interventions, 14*(4), 223−231. https://doi.org/10.1002/(sici)1099-078x(199910/12)14:4<223::aid-bin37>3.0.co;2-y.

Cooper, J. O., Heron, T. E., & Heward, W. L. (2020). *Applied behavior analysis*. Pearson.

Critchfield, T. S. (2015). What counts as high-quality practitioner training in applied behavior analysis? *Behavior Analysis in Practice, 8*(1), 3−6. https://doi.org/10.1007/s40617-015-0049-0.

Eldridge, P. (1966). *Seven against the night*. Yoseloff.

El Fattal, R. (2022, May 23). Robbie El Fattal, Ph.D., BCBA-D *with* Amy L. Odum, Ph.D. and Jonathan Tarbox, Ph.D., BCBA-D (Video). YouTube. https://www.youtube.com/watch?v=0J8iRwlr-H0&t=2019s.

Freeman, T., LeBlanc, L., & Martinez-Diaz, J. (2020). Ethical and professional responsibilities of applied behavior analysts. In J. Cooper, T. Heron, & W. Heward (Eds.), *Applied behavior analysis* (3rd ed., pp. 757−782). essay, Pearson Education.

Hanley, G. (2021, October 19). *A perspective on today's ABA from Dr. Hanley*. Practical Functional Assessment https://practicalfunctionalassessment.com/2021/09/09/a-perspective-on-todays-aba-by-dr-greg-hanley.

Harrison, A. (2019, May 23). An Open Letter to Behavior Analysis. *LinkedIN*. Retrieved September 10, 2022, from https://www.linkedin.com/pulse/open-letter-behavior-analysis-dr-antonio-harrison-bcba-d/?trackingId=%2B8H0cabjRd6IYPGQoyB6pw%3D%3D.

Kelly, A. N. (2019). E. Scott Geller on actively caring (Audio podcast episode). Behaviorbabe. https://anchor.fm/behaviorbabe/episodes/Dr−E−Scott-Geller-on-Actively-Caring-e9tp32.

Kelly, A. N. (2020a). Antonio Harrison on turning on the lights. (Audio podcast episode). Behaviorbabe. https://anchor.fm/behaviorbabe/episodes/Dr−Antonio-Harrison-on-Turning-On-the-Lights-e4o24p.

Kelly, A. N. (2020b). Jackie MacDonald on life-work balance (Audio podcast episode). Behaviorbabe. https://anchor.fm/behaviorbabe/episodes/Dr−Jackie-MacDonald-on-Life-Work-Balance-eahu3s.

Kelly, A. N. (2020c). Justin Leaf on ensuring a BRight future for our field (Audio podcast episode). Behaviorbabe. https://anchor.fm/behaviorbabe/episodes/Dr−Justin-Leaf-on-Ensuring-a-Bright-Future-for-Our-Field-ea456i.

Kelly, A. N. (2020d). Julia Fiebig on being okay with being uncomfortable. (Audio podcast episode). Behaviorbabe. https://anchor.fm/behaviorbabe/episodes/Dr−Julia-Fiebig-on-Being-Okay-with-Being-Uncomfortable-e9ojci.

Kelly, A. N. (2020e). Patricia Wright on cultural humility (Audio podcast episode). Behaviorbabe. https://anchor.fm/behaviorbabe/episodes/Dr−Patricia-Wright-on-Cultural-Humility-egq034.

Kelly, A. N. (2021). Eileen Lamb on cyberbullying in the autism community (Audio podcast episode). Behaviorbabe. https://anchor.fm/behaviorbabe/episodes/Eileen-Lamb-on-The-Autism-Cafe-e113632.

Rosenberg, N. E., & Schwartz, I. S. (2019). Guidance or compliance: What makes an ethical behavior analyst? *Behavior Analysis in Practice, 12*(2), 473−482. https://doi.org/10.1007/s40617-018-00287-5.

Taylor, B. A., LeBlanc, L. A., & Nosik, M. R. (2018). Compassionate care in behavior analytic treatment: Can outcomes be enhanced by attending to relationships with caregivers? *Behavior Analysis in Practice, 12*(3), 654−666. https://doi.org/10.1007/s40617-018-00289-3.

Wolf, M. M. (1978). Social validity: The case for subjective measurement or how applied behavior analysis is finding its heart. *Journal of Applied Behavior Analysis, 11*(2), 203–214. https://doi. org/10.1901/jaba.1978.11-203.

Wright, P. I. (2019). Cultural humility in the practice of applied behavior analysis. *Behavior Analysis in Practice, 12*(4), 805–809. https://doi.org/10.1007/s40617-019-00343-8.

Discussion questions

1. What is the relevance of the spider web on the cover of this book?
2. Which two models for ethical decision making are introduced? Who are the authors of each?
3. List the steps in the six-step model reviewed (Rosenberg and Schwartz, 2019).
4. What are the four core principles discussed in the BACB Ethics Code? Give an example of how each principle can be applied.
5. What is the relevance of taking an ethics course? Why is this a requirement for behavior analysts?

Appendix A

Six-Step Decision-Making Worksheet

1. Why does this trigger your ethical radar?

_____

_____

_____

_____

_____

_____

_____

_____

2. Brainstorm solutions.
   a. Review the BACB Ethics Code. List 2 or 3 relevant ethics strands.

_____

_____

_____

_____

_____

_____

_____

_____

   b. What did your mentors, supervisors, or peers suggest?

_____

_____

_____

_____

_____

_____

_____

   c. What does the literature say on this topic?

_____

_____

_____

_____

_____

_____

_____

This worksheet is intended to assist in ethical decision-making, as outlined by: *Rosenberg, N. E., & Schwartz, I. S. (2018). Guidance or compliance: What makes an ethical behavior analyst? Behavior Analysis in Practice, 12(2), 473–482. https://doi.org/10.1007/s40617-018-00287-5.*

d. What do other experts in the field say about this?

_____
_____
_____
_____
_____
_____
_____

3. Evaluation solutions. *(Consider what issues, conflicts, or tensions might potentially influence each solution. Consider client safety, client dignity and self-determination, client outcomes, impact on your relationships with other parties, and family preferences.)*

_____
_____
_____
_____
_____
_____
_____

4. What is the best solution? What do you feel are the next steps? List all steps you plan to take.

_____
_____
_____
_____
_____
_____
_____
_____
_____
_____
_____
_____
_____
_____
_____
_____

This worksheet is intended to assist in ethical decision-making, as outlined by: *Rosenberg, N. E., & Schwartz, I. S. (2018). Guidance or compliance: What makes an ethical behavior analyst? Behavior Analysis in Practice, 12(2), 473–482. https://doi.org/10.1007/s40617-018-00287-5.*

5. Implement the solution with fidelity and carefully document all actions taken.
6. Reflect upon the results/effects of your decision.
   a. Was it a successful resolution?

   _____
   _____
   _____

   b. Do you need to take any further steps?

   _____
   _____
   _____

   c. Have you learned anything that will affect future ethical decisions?

   _____
   _____
   _____
   _____

This worksheet is intended to assist in ethical decision-making, as outlined by: _Rosenberg, N. E., & Schwartz, I. S. (2018). Guidance or compliance: What makes an ethical behavior analyst? Behavior Analysis in Practice, 12(2), 473–482. https://doi.org/10.1007/s40617-018-00287-5._

Section 1

Responsibility as a professional

"You are personally responsible for becoming more ethical than the society you grew up in."

Eliezer Yudkowsky

Back to Basics. https://doi.org/10.1016/B978-0-323-85566-2.00002-X

Discussion Questions

1. What are the benefits to including clients and stakeholders in assessment and treatment planning?
2. How can behavior analysts and technicians stay abreast of evolving expectations in our field?
3. What must behavior analysts do when engaging in new areas of practice, when implementing new procedures, and when working with new populations?

Section 1 of the Ethics Code for Behavior Analysts addresses our responsibilities as professional. It looks at responsibilities that analysts have to be truthful, to gain and maintain competence, to be aware of biases and how they may affect a client's services, and to avoid multiple relationships. We address each of these areas in this section, with the focus remaining on the best interest of the client.

When we think of operating in the best interest of others, it may be as if we are already doing this daily. How do we know what is in the best interest of our clients and their families? One aspect of representing and supporting our clients is to engage and involve them in all aspects of the assessment process and treatment planning. By asking the client what is meaningful to them, we lower the risk of making well-intended assumptions about others' goals and desires (BACB, 2020, 1.01).

To demonstrate that we are reliable and dependable, we must behave in ways that others view as dependable and honest. Behavior analysts must take strides to be honest, even when the truth may be uncomfortable. We must also seize opportunities to correct others when they have represented our skills, credentials, claims, or abilities inaccurately. Although not every inaccuracy may be brought to light, imagine a situation in which a client (or relevant stakeholder) discovers a lie or half-truth, where you either omitted certain facts or failed to provide clarity. This experience will likely result in mistrust or uncertainty, which can have a negative and damaging impact on your relationship—and your reputation (BACB, 2020, 1.01).

The expectation for behavior analysts is that we will conform with legal and professional requirements, which include requirements set forth by the BACB, as well as requirements outlined in licensure laws and contracts with health plans. The need for a reputable professional credential was evident early in the history of our field as a mechanism to ensure proper training and has resulted in increased consumer protection. Efforts toward credentialing began in the early 1970s. Over the past several decades, a number of initiatives have been created to address the rapidly growing needs of the profession and to assist in establishing a valued professional identity. In "A History of Credentialing of Behavior Analysts" (Johnston et al., 2017) the authors take readers on a journey through the history of credentialing efforts, which ultimately led to the creation of the BACB and the following progress toward licensure at the state level in the United States.

Ignorance, or failure to know and understand the law, is not an excuse for behavior that violates these legal and professional expectations. It can be incredibly daunting and overwhelming to stay abreast of expectations, especially when they are continually evolving. This is a major reason why it is critical that we stay immersed in the literature base and with mentors and colleagues, that we join and engage with our professional associations (e.g., Council of Autism Service Providers [CASP], Association of Professional Behavior Analysts [APBA], etc.), and that we attend local and national conferences (e.g., Minnesota Association for Behavior Analysis (MNABA), Black Association for Behavior Analysis (BABA)) (BACB, 2020, 1.02). Behavior analysts may also choose to expand their scope of competence by obtaining training specific to relevant laws. For those working specifically with autistic individuals, the Autism Law Summit is an annual gathering of self-advocates, caregivers, providers, payors, and attorneys—all of whom dedicate their careers to enhancing access and outcomes for individuals with autism. These conferences and resources have the intention of increasing our knowledge and awareness of the frequently changing expectations of us as professional behavior analysts.

Another responsibility of behavior analysts is being accountable to our clients for our actions. Mistakes will happen and oversights do occur; when they do, we must take responsibility for our actions and take all steps necessary to "directly address them, first in the best interest of our clients, and then in the best interest of relevant parties" (BACB, 2020, 1.03). A popular quote by B. F. Skinner captures the beauty of making mistakes. In his words, he notes, "A failure is not always a mistake, it may simply be the best one can do under the circumstances. The real mistake is to stop trying" (Skinner, 1971, p. 153). While the conversations around mistakes and oversights may be uncomfortable, they are essential to creating and maintaining a collaborative working relationship.

It can be tempting to offer our services whenever we see a child in need, but unless a contract is signed for us to provide support, we must refrain from providing advice or treatment. As noted in the BACB Ethics Code, "Behavior analysts provide services only after defining and documenting their professional role with relevant parties in writing" (2020, 1.04).

Callout Box 1:

You are consulting for a classroom in a local school district. When you are there to provide support for your client, the teacher tells you on your way out the door that the principal would like to talk to you about another student. When you stop by the principal's office, she asks that you stop in a neighboring classroom when you are on campus tomorrow and provide some strategies for a student in that room. You tell the principal you would be happy to assist, as long as you have consent from the family to collaborate on this child's team. The principal assures you they will get consent when they meet with the caregivers next. She reiterates the severity of the behavior and asks that you stop in tomorrow to see if there are any recommendations you can provide in the interim to the teacher for this student.

Referring to Scenario 1, let us begin by asking ourselves "What is the potential harm to the client?" In this case, the risk of harm to the client is high if you begin intervening or assessing without proper written consent. You want to ensure that the client is protected—and that you are as well. Once you obtain written consent, you can refer to this document if anyone asks if the family is aware of your involvement. Although the family can revoke its permission at any time, no services should begin until the analyst receives informed written consent for assessment and treatment. It is incredibly important to follow the rules issued by the BACB, and to be aware of applicable laws and regulations that may also pertain to a particular situation. Under the Individuals with Disabilities Education Act (IDEA), there are protections for children with special needs, which include the right to written consent before the creation of a behavior plan or treatment plan. You can consult with a local attorney or contact your state department of education (DOE) to learn more about the rights of children in school settings so that you can prepare yourself to advocate on behalf of the client.

Continuing with our inquiry, by referring to several sections of the Code we can answer the question "What does it mean to be a 'good' behavior analyst?" For example, our ethical obligations for "conforming with legal and professional requirements" (BACB, 2020, 1.02), practicing in a defined role (1.04), obtaining informed consent (2.11), and ensuring a signed service agreement before implementing services (3.04) allow us to maintain responsibility to clients (3.01).

Last, let us ask ourselves "What is the right thing to do?" With so much overlapping and overwhelming guidance coming directly from our ethical code, the right thing to do would be to support the principal and school team in obtaining consent for assessment and/or treatment. You may wish to offer to reach out to the family on behalf of the school or to meet with the family to explain the consent form and assessment process. It is equally important for us to maintain a healthy relationship with the caregivers, as recipients of our services, and the school team, who are the persons seeking our help.

Why is it important for behavior analysts to practice only within their defined area of competence (BACB, 2020, 1.05; Kelly, 2019)? There are probably some common-sense answers to this question, as well as some that are a little more nuanced. What do we mean by saying we are competent? Some adjectives that come to mind are fluent, well practiced, experienced, trained, and comfortable. When we take on a client, we are communicating that we feel safe implementing the recommended procedures and we possess the competence to develop and oversee their programming. When engaging in new areas of practice, implementing new procedures, and working with new populations, behavior analysts must only do so after "accessing and documenting appropriate study, training, supervised experience, consultation, and/or co-treatment from professionals competent in the new area" (1.05). In a

Behaviorbabe podcast, Rachel Taylor talks about "defining the magic" of behavior change, which includes practicing within our scope of competence and extending our scope to new populations and across age groups (Kelly, 2019). Taylor provides insight and advice for newly minted analysts, as well as for more seasoned analysts in the field, including prioritizing organizations and agencies whose values align with our own.

If we are unable to do the work to ensure our competence in a new area, then we must uphold the ethical expectation that we will refer the client to another analyst or transition services to another appropriate professional. But what do you do when you are not in charge of clients others assign to you?

Callout Box 2:

You are working for an ABA agency, where clients are assigned to you as availability opens on your schedule. Let's say you are one year postcertification, working for an agency that assigns you an 18-year-old client who has a diagnosis of oppositional defiant disorder (ODD). While obtaining your supervised fieldwork experience and in your first year as an analyst, you have only worked with clients ages two to six who have a diagnosis on the autism spectrum. You feel woefully unprepared and are extremely anxious about taking on this new client. What should you do? Use the six-step decision-making process to outline your options and determine the best course of action. Take into consideration the need to balance your current skill set with your obligation for professional development and growth. What might be two or three acceptable outcomes in this scenario?

When it comes to competency as a behavior analyst, our responsibility is ongoing. It is likely that there are going to be several moments throughout your career when you feel the challenge to expand and further develop competence with new areas of practice when implementing new procedures and when working with new populations. Practicing within our scope of competence (1.05) and maintaining competence (1.06) is something that pertains to both analysts working early in their career, as well as more seasoned analysts, which is why behavior analysts must "engage in professional development activities to maintain and further their professional competence" (BACB, 2020). Take for example the case of assessment tools, which may be developed, refined, and revised after your initial certification (e.g., VB-MAPP, Socially Savvy, PEAK, etc.). What you learned during your coursework may have prepared you for practice at the time of your studies and graduation; however, that alone is not enough, as behavior analysts have an ethical obligation to remain current and "continually evaluate and improve their . . . repertoire through professional development" (4.02), which includes "reading relevant literature; attending conferences and conventions; participating in workshops and other training opportunities; obtaining additional coursework; receiving coaching, consultation, supervision, or mentorship; and obtaining and maintaining appropriate professional credentials" (BACB, 2020, 1.05).

Behavior analysis is the study of behavior and is largely under the influence of what is important and relevant to us individually—and to society—at the time of our involvement, which is not to say that behavior analysts and behavior analysis cannot be progressive; we and it certainly can be. However, behavior analysts are humans, which means we make mistakes. Like our clients, their families, and others, we also are under the influence of our environment. Thus, what is relevant to society will directly impact what we consider to be worthy of investigation, support, and intervention. As a profession, we take our cues and clues from current events and seek to continually evolve and elevate our practices as they relate to the application of the science of behavior analysis.

As behavior analysts, we must actively engage in activities that increase our awareness and responsiveness to cultural diversity (BACB, 2020, 1.07). This could include attending workshops and reading formal publications on the topic; however, it may also include volunteering in various communities. When we speak of addressing behaviors and challenges relevant to a particular community, we must first learn the priorities of that community. "Ethical and moral principles have undoubtedly been valuable in the design of cultural practices" (Skinner, 1965, p. 445). If we limit our perspectives to only the experiences we have individually, we miss opportunities to honor and value the perspectives of others, which likely differ from our own. Behavior analysts must evaluate our "own biases and ability to address the needs of individuals with diverse needs/backgrounds" (BACB, 2020, 1.07). Consider goals relating to eating, such as independence with feeding, expanding food repertoires, and proper utensil use. The way you will approach these skills will be dependent on the culture and context. Imagine teaching a child not to eat with their hands in a culture where eating with their hands is the norm, as it is in some communities in Southeast Asia. For clients who live in warm, tropical climates, focusing on shoe tying is likely less important than for clients who live in colder climates, such as in New England, whereas learning to tie fishing line or bathing suit strings might be applicable in both communities.

As analysts, we also evaluate potential biases of our supervisees and trainees. Our biases and our assumptions can impact the grace we give others, which may not always be equitable or fair. It is important to create an awareness of our biases and to adjust our behavior accordingly. To address the influence of our reinforcement and punishment histories (e.g., biases) in our consultative and supervisory relationships, without prejudice, we must first learn to evaluate and acknowledge our experiences and the potential influence of these experiences on our clients. Even well-intended analysts will make mistakes or missteps; doing so is natural and a part of being a perfectly imperfect human being.

Callout Box 3:

You are working in an in-home setting and during every session your client's grandmother offers you scones. You politely decline and continue with your session. The grandmother interrupts each session, asking numerous times if you are well fed and if she can prepare any food for you. What would you do?

Referring to Scenario 3, whether you wish to consume the item or not, simply refusing the offer may be harmful to the client-provider relationship. Clients and stakeholders may view this seemingly small gesture of declining food as brutally and culturally offensive. The question to ask oneself is whether declining the item is more harmful and potentially more damaging to the relationship than accepting the item would have been, even if you choose to place it in your bag and not eat the item during the session.

In addition to being culturally aware, sensitive, and responsive, behavior analysts must also be cognizant not to discriminate against others. We have an ethical obligation to behave in a way that others consider "equitable and inclusive" regardless of various factors (BACB, 2020, 1.08).

Callout Box 4:

You collaborate and work with several colleagues of varying backgrounds and histories. On a video call, others observe you being a bit abrupt with one team member. This team member happens to be the only one of a particular gender on the call. While you may be responding to the individual regardless of gender, we must still ask ourselves these questions: "How is this dynamic influencing our decision making?" "Would we behave this way toward another colleague who is behaving in the same way regardless of their gender, age, status within the company, and so on?" "What can we do to test and challenge these beliefs?" "What steps can we take to ensure we are operating with equitable compassion and curiosity toward all our colleagues—and clients?"

Along the same lines, there is the expectation that behavior analysts will avoid engaging in behavior that is harassing or hostile toward others (BACB, 2020, 1.09). While it can be challenging to be collegial with those who have expressed opposing ideas, we should welcome those who, professionally and politely, challenge the status quo. When we refer to collaboration, we think of "working together for a common goal or collectively striving to achieve change" (Kelly, 2018). Again, we are human and capable of making (and learning from our) mistakes, and we also must recognize a shared commitment to operate in the best interest of our clients. By reminding ourselves that we have a shared, centralized goal, we help set the stage for collaboration toward compassionate and kind outcomes for our clients—and our colleagues (1.09). However, many factors impact collaboration, several of which are beyond our control, including the type of collaboration (e.g., educational, medical, legal, etc.), the age of team members, the history and length of time associates are in their current position or with the current company, and the level of training of each team member (Kelly, 2018). While a diverse team is highly desirable, it also comes with diverse thinking, which can create a conflict or cause friction (McCullough, 2018). When disagreements occur, particularly in the workplace, it is common to reach out to trusted coworkers to vent or express our frustrations. However, doing so can be dangerous and destructive, as it may encourage coworkers to weigh in and take sides. It is perfectly understandable and advisable to seek support. However, it is recommended that you reach out to colleagues outside your current agency in order to reduce additional friction among team members.

Perhaps the biggest and toughest step we can take is to maintain "awareness that [our] personal biases or challenges (e.g., mental or physical health conditions; legal, financial, marital/relationship challenges) may interfere with our ability to be effective professionally" (BACB, 2020, p. 4). When situations arise, which could compete with our professional responsibilities, we must take "appropriate steps to resolve interference, [and to] ensure that [our] professional work is not compromised" (BACB, 2020, 1.10).

Callout Box 5:

You are working as a behavior analyst for an ABA agency and your spouse has recently announced they wish to file for divorce. This comes on the heels of the news that your elderly mother received a recent diagnosis of Alzheimer's. While your personal life may be understandably overwhelming, you feel like you are able to focus on your clients. Over time, caregivers begin commenting to your employer that you have missed several sessions, which has compromised the reauthorization of service hours for the most recent treatment for at least one of your clients. What should you do now, considering the impact of your actions on your clients? What can be done to prevent the impact on your clients? What creative ways can you conceptualize protecting your clients, while honoring your need to grieve and heal balanced with your need to maintain a healthy income to sustain your livelihood and to provide for your children?

Multiple relationships occur when there is a "commingling of two or more of a behavior analyst's roles with a client, stakeholder, supervisee, trainee, research participant, or someone closely associated with or related to the client" (BACB, 2020, 1.11). For a multiple relationship to occur, the behavior analyst must serve in both roles at once. This could look, for example, like a client of yours joining the little league team you coach where you are not acting in the capacity of the client's behavior analyst. When multiple relationships arise, we have an ethical obligation to take steps to resolve them and, if immediate resolution is not possible, we are responsible for putting into place "appropriate safeguards to identify and avoid conflicts of interest" (BACB, 2020, 1.11). As with all other things, the expectation is that we will document all actions taken, as well as the ultimate outcomes we achieve. It is important to realize that this code pertains to our colleagues as well as our clients.

Callout Box 6:

You are a behavior analyst who works at an agency that provides ABA services to children. As part of your work responsibilities, you also supervise individuals pursuing certification. Your boss approaches you about taking on a new supervisee, who happens to be his wife. You are uncomfortable saying no, but you also worry this will negatively impact your performance evaluation at work. In this case, your boss's wife is your superior's spouse, your colleague, and now potentially your supervisee.

Referring to Scenario 6, it is clear to see that this situation constitutes a multiple relationship, which inherently presents an increased risk for conflicts of interest. As noted in the scenario, you are uncomfortable being honest and advocating in the best interest of all stakeholders, which compromises your ability to be an effective analyst. Perhaps the larger question to explore here is whether it is appropriate for your boss's wife, the one who is pursuing certification, to do so at her current place of employment. If securing an alternative practicum placement is not possible, another option might be to hire someone outside of the company, whose sole purpose is to provide supervisory support to this individual. Either way, in this case you will want to share your concerns with your boss. You may find success in referencing the Ethics Code when suggesting alternative solutions and by making appropriate referrals to other potential supervisors. It is imperative for us to speak our truths, even when we are uncomfortable doing so.

Whenever we discuss ethics and multiple relationships, it is inevitable that someone will bring up the question of what constitutes a gift. Specifically, the question that arises frequently is if we can accept a glass of water.

Callout Box 7:

You are working an 8-hour day, which is split between two clients who receive their services in-home, across town from one another. Most days, you bring a bottle of water with you. However, today you forgot. You mention being thirsty in the presence of the caregiver, who offers you a fresh bottle of water. Could accepting the water be classified as accepting a gift? Will this behavior constitute a multiple relationship? Will drinking the water present a conflict of interest?

Let us be the first to tell you our ethical code has nothing to do with a glass of water and everything to do with the relationship that is potentially being formed. In the scenario described, there is little to no harm to the client if an analyst or technician accepts a bottle of water. The client is not directly impacted by this action, and there does not appear to be any negative indirect impacts either. A "good" behavior analyst would focus, after accepting the bottle of water with a smile, on the client's programs and session. The right thing to do is to say thank you, accept the water, and move on with the services you are there to provide. Now, imagine a slightly different scenario where feelings are hurt because you do not accept what is offered.

Callout Box 8:

You are working an 8-hour day that is split between two clients who receive their services in-home, across town from one another. You mention being tired in the presence of the caregiver, who offers you coffee. You hesitate but then decide that accepting the coffee is less problematic than falling asleep during your session. At your next session, the caregiver has a cup of coffee poured for you. However, today you had time to stop between sessions, and you brought your own coffee. The caregiver seems a little annoyed, commenting that they had bought the flavored creamer you had said you like. You offer your thanks for the coffee and say that there is no need to provide coffee for you in the future. The caregiver approaches the table where you are sitting with the client, picks up the cup of coffee, and pours it down the drain while exhaling an exasperated sigh.

Contrasting Scenarios 7 and 8, it is easy to see that the actions of the individual in Scenario 7 resulted in a positive continued relationship, with the needs of the client quickly attended to, whereas in Scenario 8 there may be a negative interaction between the caregiver and the analyst due to refusing the coffee. Accepting water or a cup of coffee by itself does not mean a multiple relationship has formed, though the refusal of the coffee does nonetheless appear to be problematic for the therapeutic relationship. This illustrates why it is important to look not only at the action but also to consider the impact on the professional relationship. Accepting and giving gifts can lead to the development of a nonprofessional relationship, and when more than one relationship occurs simultaneously, there is the potential for conflicts of interest to occur. Witts and colleagues delved deeper into the phenomenon of gift giving in the field of behavior analysis in an article titled "Behavior Analysts Accept Gifts During Practice: So Now What?" (Witts et al., 2020). Although this article explores behavior analysts accepting gifts during a time when the BACB fully prohibited gifts, the lessons learned through their inquiry still apply today. The article offers insight as to how some may justify accepting gifts, despite limitations imposed by the BACB. Over time, the BACB has revised its statement on gifts, which now permits gifts under $10, when they function as an "infrequent expression of gratitude" and do not "result in financial benefit to the recipient" (BACB, 2020, 1.12). There are additional restrictions and limitations surrounding the conditions under which receiving or giving gifts is ethically appropriate. Where there are limitations, ethical dilemmas and tricky situations lie ahead, and the Witts article explores some of these situations and the potential implications.

The best way to respond to a problem is to prevent it from occurring. We can accomplish this by being familiar with the Ethics Code (and its subsequent revisions) and by making clients aware of its contents at the onset of a professional relationship. To go one step further, you can encourage your organization to include information in client intake paperwork about gifts and our responsibility as BACB certificants to prevent multiple relationships and conflicts of interest from occurring.

Callout Box 9:

You are working as an assistant behavior analyst for a relatively small organization. About a year into working for this organization, you have the opportunity to work one on one with a client in a public-school setting. You want to take the position; however, it is a bit farther away from the clinic, and with the increased cost associated with mileage it is not feasible for you to accept the position. The father of the client learns of this and wants to help. He asks what part of the town you live in and if there is anything he can do. You thank him for his interest, tell him where your apartment complex is, and assure him you will try to work something out. A few weeks later, on a Friday, you get a letter from the manager of your rental company saying that they are lowering your rent by $200 a month. There is no reason provided. You ask your neighbors if they received a similar letter. They received a letter, notifying them of a rental increase of $100 starting next month. They are upset with you for what feels like preferential treatment. You think about looking more into it, but then shrug it off. A few days later, you tell your agency you will take the position. On your first day at dropoff, the father makes a comment saying he is happy you took the job after all. He mentions talking to the manager of your rental property, saying something about being former college buddies. You realize the father "pulled some strings" so you could work with his child. In response to his comments, you smile and walk with your client into the classroom.

In Scenario 9, a direct kickback was given to you as the analyst so you would accept working with this client. If the father had not used his influence to get your rent lowered, you would have been unable to work for his child. While you did not ask for or accept a gift, a multiple relationship and conflict of interest exists. The potential for harm in this situation is great. What else will the father expect in return? Will you be obligated to pay back the reduced rent if you leave the company? What is your obligation if you are assigned to another client? Good behavior analysts would recognize the potential problems associated with this exchange and would immediately inform their employer. Although the analyst should thank the family and let them know their generosity is appreciated, it creates a conflict and an uncomfortable working situation for the analyst.

Hopefully, you will work for an organization that will support and reinforce your honesty and transparency. It is a huge testament to your professional skills that the family wants you to work with their child. If your organization values this request, they may want to reevaluate your worth to the organization and reflect it in your financial compensation. We all deserve to make a respectable, livable wage and to do so by behaving ethically.

When working with clients and their families in intimate settings and through emotional experiences, it is increasingly likely that a multiple relationship will develop.

Callout Box 10:

A client is receiving 20 hours a week of ABA services. The medical recommendation is for services to occur across settings, but the family is only interested in having in-home sessions, 4 hours a day. Due to staffing limitations and parental preference, only one technician is available to provide all 20 hours of care each week. There is no plan for adding an additional technician. What is the potential for harm?

Situations in which one provider is responsible for all of the treatment hours or remains on a case for many years may establish the perfect conditions for conflicts to occur. They may also bring about missed opportunities to program for generalization for our clients. Another setback is that we are not allowing the technician the opportunity to work with multiple clients so they can further develop and refine their skills. A "good" behavior analyst would see this as a potential breeding ground for conflict. The right thing to do would be to have multiple technicians assigned to work with the client. Another option would be to consider shifting the treatment location to include the clinic, community, or school setting.

As behavior analysts we must be certain that we do not engage in any behavior or practices that are coercive or exploitative (BACB, 2020, 1.13). Ethically, we are prohibited from using our power to exploit those we have authority over. We have been given an opportunity to help individuals, whether they are a client, a relevant stakeholder, or a supervisee, and we must not betray this trust. "Behavior analysts do not engage in romantic or sexual relationships with current clients, stakeholders, trainees, or supervisees" (BACB, 2020, 1.14).

Callout Box 11:

You are working as a supervisor for a client receiving in-home services. You occasionally flirt with the neighbor, who eventually asks you out on a date. You check in with yourself and decide it is not a problem because the neighbor is neither the client nor a family member of the client. You go on a few dates, then the neighbor stops calling. You feel embarrassed and avoid going to the client's house for supervision, worried you will run into the neighbor. Eventually you ask for the case to be reassigned to another analyst, but there is no one available to take over for a few weeks. Since you are not comfortable going to the house, the company places the client's services on hold until a new supervisor can begin.

In Scenario 11, the client was harmed as a direct result of your actions. Assuming you are ethically in the clear to date the neighbor of a client, you are also ethically obligated and responsible for ensuring ongoing access to services. In this case, the technician was not appropriately supervised, as you were uncomfortable going to the home for sessions after being ghosted by the neighbor. While you took the appropriate steps to ask for the case to be reassigned, you did not assume responsibility for ensuring continuity of services and a seamless transition for the client. The right thing to do would have been to either not go on a date with the neighbor, overcoming discomfort and continuing to provide supervision of the technician, and/or to ask for a transfer and remain on the case until an appropriate transfer could occur. We must remember that behavior analysts operate first and foremost in the best interest of our clients.

With former clients and stakeholders, behavior analysts must wait "for a period of two years after the professional relationship has ended" before embarking on a romantic or sexual relationship. For former supervisees and trainees, behavior analysts must document that the professional relationship has ended (BACB, 2020, 1.14).

Callout Box 12:

You are a professor who teaches undergraduate and graduate classes. You realize you have an attraction to one of your students, and the feeling appears to be mutual. Your student tells you they are interested in you sexually. You tell your student you think they are cute, but you cannot date students, despite the attraction. Six months later, the student graduates, obtains certification as a behavior analyst, and moves out of state. Several years later, you run into your former student at a conference. You talk for hours and have several drinks before you both head back to your room, where you spend the night together.

In Scenario 12, you may have teetered on inappropriate behavior by telling your student you were physically attracted to them; however, no sexual or romantic relationship existed until after the professional relationship had ended. Presuming several years is at least two years later, this behavior is not unethical by current standards. Some may not condone the behavior and it may go against personal values, but it does not seem to violate our ethical code.

Callout Box 13:

Considering Scenario 12, let us look forward a few months into the future. Two months after returning from your conference travels, your university is hiring for a director of online learning. One of the applications in the stack of résumés was submitted by your former student who you recently reconnected with at the conference hotel. Before moving forward with the interviews, what steps should you take?

The potential for harm in Scenario 13 is significant because it impacts your new potential hire and also all students this individual will oversee and supervise. Ethically, behavior analysts have an ethical obligation and must refrain from entering a professional relationship with any "supervisees or trainees with whom they have had a past romantic or sexual relationship for at least six months after the relationship has ended" (BACB, 2020, 1.14). In this case, you can make known your past sexual relationship and excuse yourself from the interview or hiring committee. However, would doing so create a situation where this specific candidate could be discriminated against because of their sexual prowess? Again, we have a situation in which the answer is neither black nor white but, rather, one of the many shades of gray. As analysts, we cannot allow the actions we take to negatively impact our clients, and that extends to our students, supervisees, and trainees. We must take our roles seriously and revere the responsibility we possess.

One of the best ways we can set up our clients for success is to set up ourselves for success. This means being familiar with our Ethics Code, as well as community standards and local, state, and federal laws affecting the practice of behavior analysis. Being familiar with the rights and prerogatives of our clients allows us to ensure protections of their rights to the best of our ability. Behavior analysts who provide services that are funded by health insurance must educate themselves about laws such as the Mental Health Parity Addiction and Equity Act (MHPAEA), which asserts that health plans cannot place limitations on mental health disorders that are not also placed on physical injuries or disabilities. For example, if a health plan does not require physicians to cut a patient's cast off their broken arm when they turn 15 years of age, then they legally cannot stop covering ABA at the age of 15 (or any other age). Similarly, health plans cannot discontinue coverage of ABA arbitrarily at age 15 (or any other age) for individuals diagnosed with autism, which is defined by the DSM-5 as a mental health condition. Some believe that age and dollar caps are violations, and recently it has been suggested that funders cannot impose these restrictions in states that define ABA as an *essential health benefit*. If you are a business owner, or someone who is engaging in contract negotiations, it is critical for you to be aware of laws such as the Sherman Antitrust Act, which prohibits the discussion of negotiated rates with other providers in the same space. If you are supporting a client in an educational setting, you will likely need to understand laws pertaining to Individualized Education Programs (IEPs), which you can find in your state's procedural guidelines, which schools are required to provide to caregivers and legal guardians. When we possess knowledge about community standards, laws, regulations, and rules, we are in the best position to advocate for our clients and their right to access effective behavioral treatment.

As analysts, we are also expected to "adhere to practice requirements imposed by the BACB, our employers, and governmental entities" (BACB, 2020, 1.15), in very much the same way as other regulated mental health professionals do (e.g., psychologists, social workers, marriage and family therapists, etc.). In addition, we must remain knowledgeable about our ethics and practice requirements, which include "compliance with self-reporting requirements" (1.16).

The BACB has created a checklist for evaluating when to make a self-report. Items on this checklist include asking oneself if you have committed an ethical violation or are the subject of an investigation or legal civil actions. If you have a mentor or supervisor, the BACB suggests discussing with them first the need to self-report (BACB, 2020). We will provide more information regarding the self-reporting process toward the end of this text. We always recommend visiting the BACB website for the most current, up-to-date information.

Callout Box 14:

You learn that the organization where you have been working has submitted fraudulent claims under your name to health plans. Essentially, your signature was forged, and the health plans were charged for services you did not provide. In this case, your employer has engaged in egregious acts and has put you and your clients at risk. You have not committed any violations or broken any laws, per se, but an investigation would show your name on the fraudulent claims. What steps should you take? What is your obligation for reporting this to the BACB?

As noted previously in the Introduction and Roadmap, some situations clearly constitute ethical violations, particularly those in which laws have been broken. Referring to the six-step decision-making process outlined by Rosenberg and Schwartz (2019), misrepresentation of our services, as in Scenario 14, immediately raises a red flag. Steps 2 and 3 lead us to brainstorming ideas and evaluating solutions. A quick walk-through of the ethical code reveals that billing fraudulently is a violation with a clear and prescribed course of action (step 4). In this case, you must approach your employer. Consider the possibility that this is also occurring for other analysts and their clients. Also consider the possibility that this may have been an error or mistake, or possibly that this was done without your employer's knowledge. After you discuss the matter with your employer, you must inform the health plan as well as any relevant authorities. You must also inform your client, so they may follow up with their health plan to ensure that they did not pay for services that you did not provide, as the billing sheets indicate. Regarding whether you need to contact the BACB or not, visit and review the updated information on its website regarding self-reporting. If you remain unsure after doing so, we suggest defaulting to contacting the board. Imagine what may happen if you do not.

Imagine after informing your employer that your name has been used to fraudulently bill that they decide to fault you and terminate your employment. A few weeks later, you receive notification from the BACB that your employer has filed an ethics complaint against you, which is what will be used against you in the determination to fire you due to evidence of wrongdoing. If you have already informed the BACB of the information you uncover, the BACB will view your employer's complaint in the context of the information you provided, which is helpful when determining the role you played in the situation. If you chose not to alert the BACB, you may still be able to demonstrate that you were not at fault for submitting fraudulent claims; however, you may have violated the BACB's requirements around self-reporting. After implementing the solution (step 5), remember step 6: reflect upon results. Did the situation resolve itself as you would have liked? What steps can you can take in the future to ensure that this does not occur again? Would you do anything differently if you found yourself in a similar situation?

Section 1 of the Ethics Code speaks to our responsibility as professionals, which encompasses behaving with integrity, committing to developing our competences, creating awareness of personal biases, and establishing appropriate professional boundaries. It is imperative that we maintain our commitment to upholding these ethical expectations. Doing so will likely involve intentional and frequent self-reflection. When facing certain situations, the answers will immediately reveal themselves; more often, answers will be harder to find and will require further investigation.

References

Behavior Analyst Certification Board (BACB). (2020). Ethics code for behavior analysts. https://bacb.com/wp-content/ethics-code-for-behavior-analysts.

Johnston, J. M., Carr, J. E., & Mellichamp, F. H. (2017). A history of the professional credentialing of applied behavior analysts. *The Behavior Analyst, 40*(2), 523−538. https://doi.org/10.1007/s40614-017-0106-9.

Kelly, A. N. (2018, April). When professionals disagree: The ethics of effective collaboration. West Coast Conference on Autism. Buellton; California. http://www.behavior.org/resources/1034.pdf.

Kelly, A. N. (Host). (2019). Rachel Taylor on defining the magic (Audio podcast episode). *Behaviorbabe.* https://anchor.fm/behaviorbabe/episodes/Dr—Rachel-Taylor-on-Defining-the-Magic-e3l4r8.

McCullough, R. (2018). *Insider intelligence: Conflict in the workplace.* Security Info Watch. https://www.securityinfowatch.com/integrators/article/12399219/conflict-in-the-workplace. Retrieved July 20, 2022.

Rosenberg, N. E., & Schwartz, I. S. (2019). Guidance or compliance: What makes an ethical behavior analyst? *Behavior Analysis in Practice, 12*(2), 473—482. https://doi.org/10.1007/s40617-018-00287-5.

Self-reporting statement - BACB. Behavior Analyst Certification Board. (2021, December). https://www.bacb.com/wp-content/uploads/2021/12/Self-Reporting-Statement-211228.pdf. Retrieved May 30, 2022.

Skinner, B. F. (1965). *Science and human behavior.* Free Press.

Skinner, B. F. (1971). *Beyond Freedom and dignity.* Richard Clay. The Chaucer Press.

Witts, B. N., Brodhead, M. T., Adlington, L. C., & Barron, D. K. (2020). Behavior analysts accept gifts during practice: So now what? *Behavior Analysis: Research and Practice, 20*(3), 196—202. https://doi.org/10.1037/bar0000117.

Discussion questions

1. What are the benefits to including clients and stakeholders in assessment and treatment planning?
2. How can behavior analysts and technicians stay abreast of evolving expectations in our field?
3. What must behavior analysts do when engaging in new areas of practice, when implementing new procedures, and when working with new populations?
4. How can behavior analysts and technicians learn the priorities of the communities they serve?
5. Why is it important for analysts and technicians to maintain awareness of their personal biases?
6. How can behavior analysts support their perspectives when discussing ethical dilemmas with their supervisors and colleagues?
7. According to the authors, what is the best way to respond to a problem?
8. Why might an analyst or technician ask an employer to include information about aspects of the Ethics Code in client paperwork?
9. How can behavior analysts decrease the potential of dual relationships and conflicts of interest?
10. In whose best interest do behavior analysts operate first and foremost?

Section 2

Responsibility in practice

"Ethics is knowing the difference between what you have a right to do and what is right to do."

Potter Stewart

Discussion questions
1. What are the six rights of clients regarding effective behavioral treatment?
2. Why might you teach a client to expand their repertoire of preferred activities (e.g., songs)?
3. What steps might a behavior analyst take to decrease the likelihood of distress for their clients?

Back to Basics. https://doi.org/10.1016/B978-0-323-85566-2.00003-1

Section 2 of our Ethics Code focuses on our responsibilities to consumers and others as we practice as professional behavior analysts. The focus of this section is on our responsibilities to accurately and in a timely manner document services, protect the privacy of our clients, involve clients and caregivers in discussions surrounding treatment, collaborate with others in the client's life, and provide effective treatment that includes considering medical needs and taking steps to minimize any possible risk of treatment. In doing all of those things, we as behavior analysts need to keep our focus on the four core principles discussed in the Introduction and Roadmap: benefit others; treat others with compassion, dignity, and respect; behave with integrity; and ensure competence (BACB, 2020).

As behavior analysts, we must "prioritize clients' rights and needs in service delivery" (BACB, 2020, 2.01). We do this by involving clients and relevant stakeholders in discussions involving treatment selection, implementation, and outcomes. When we encounter disagreements with members of a treatment team, we must work diligently and swiftly to resolve conflicts for the sake of our clients. Disagreements result in delays in accessing effective treatment, which is an inherent right of all clients (3.14). While we must take into consideration the needs of various stakeholders (e.g., caregivers, funder requirements, etc.), we must keep the client at the core of these conversations and decisions. In a 1988 publication, "The Right to Effective Behavioral Treatment," Van Houten and colleagues detail six rights of clients who receive behavior analytic services. These include the (1) right to a therapeutic environment, (2) right to services where the overriding goal is personal welfare, (3) right to treatment by a competent behavior analyst, (4) right to programs that teach functional skills, (5) right to behavioral assessment and ongoing evaluation, and (6) right to the most effective treatment procedures available.

The Right to Effective Behavioral Treatment

@Behaviorbabe

01 RIGHT TO A THERAPEUTIC ENVIRONMENT

SERVICES WHERE THE OVERRIDING GOAL IS PERSONAL WELFARE 02

03 TREATMENT BY A COMPETENT BEHAVIOR ANALYST

PROGRAMS THAT TEACH FUNCTIONAL SKILLS 04

05 BEHAVIORAL ASSESSMENT AND ONGOING EVALUATION

THE MOST EFFECTIVE TREATMENT PROCEDURES AVAILABLE. 06

Van Houten, R., Axelrod, S., Bailey, J. S., Favell, J. E., Foxx,b R. M., Iwata, B. A., & Lovaas, O. I. (1988). The right to effective behavioral treatment. The Behavior analyst, 11(2), 111–114. https://doi.org/10.1007/BF03392464

Van Houten et al. (1988) define a therapeutic environment as "a physical and social environment which is safe, humane, and responsive to an individual's needs" (p. 381). These environments must include access to effective services, recreational activities, and materials that clients prefer and are also productive for achieving outcomes we collectively identify. We want to take into consideration client preferences as well as the age appropriateness of the materials that we are using, which includes reinforcers.

Callout Box 15:

You are working with a 10-year-old client who likes to listen to a particular song on repeat. The song he most strongly prefers is from a children's show, geared toward toddlers and preschool-age children. This fact does not bother your client, but the caregiver has mentioned that it is embarrassing to your client's brother, especially when he has friends at the house. The caregiver shared with you that one of the friends asked "Why does your brother listen to this music? Why does he listen to something so babyish?" The caregiver shared that the child was not trying to be rude or offputting but appeared sincerely inquisitive and seemed curious as to why his friend's older brother would enjoy music geared toward younger children. As an analyst, how would you respond to the caregiver?

Using Scenario 15, let us ask ourselves "What is the right thing to do?" In this case, the client seems unfazed by the comments of his brother's friends. However, the client also appears to have a limited repertoire of reinforcers, including preferred songs and activities. Furthermore, other individuals in the client's environment find his preferences unrelatable, potentially creating a barrier or challenge for increasing social interactions for your client.

The next question we must ask ourselves is "What is worth doing?" Again, the answer is not as cut and dry as it may seem at first. The right thing to do is to prioritize the client, to maintain and bring joy into the client's life, to create opportunities for interactions and engagement in natural environments, to establish a wide array of preferred and reinforcing activities, and to promote a high quality of life. While there is more than one way to approach most situations, some possibilities may yield a more favorable result than others. Let us assume you decide to expose your client to other songs, while allowing them to continue to access their favorite song, which brings them great joy. Before you design and implement an intervention, you decide to conduct an informal assessment. You explore the following question: Are there other songs that are similar that the client is willing to listen to, and what aspect of the song does the client prefer? Think back to what you learned about pairing and establishing stimulus control. Think back to the Premack Principle and decide to share your idea with the family, which is to find songs that are similar in beat to the preferred song and to ask your client to listen to the new song (or possibly portions of the song), then playing that favorite song multiple times immediately after, if desired. What is the potential for harm? There does not appear to be any; however, as analysts we are responsible for regularly conducting an assessment of the effectiveness of our programs. If we detect any distress or if the program is not working as we intend, we can stop or change direction. To decrease the likelihood of distress, we continue to provide choices to our client and are willing to adjust and adapt our programming as needed.

In addition, we are encouraged to ask ourselves "What does it mean to be a good behavior analyst?" A "good" behavior analyst would prioritize the client and the client's preferences while also being sensitive to the impact on the family. Keeping our client at the core of the conversation, we ask "How can we provide opportunities for the client to expand the repertoire of preferred items and activities?" We do not need to remove or take away something that brings joy to the client—to do so, one could argue, would be inhumane or lacking compassion, at the very least. However, we can ask if we can create opportunities to expand the client's repertoire of preferred items and activities by exposing them to a variety of songs, items, and activities.

When we talk about giving clients access to a therapeutic environment, we want to include caregivers, teachers, and team members who are responsible for competent, responsive, and caring interventions. We also want an environment that has frequent positive interactions directed toward an enjoyment of learning and fosters independence for the client. A true therapeutic environment occurs in the least restrictive setting possible while also ensuring the safety and development for each individual (Van Houten ct al., 1988). This step is important for direct-level technicians, as well as behavior analysts who are designing and overseeing programs, to recognize. Behavior analysts and direct-level technicians must minimize the use of certain items as potential reinforcers. As stated in earlier iterations of our code, we must avoid the unnecessary use of reinforcers "which could be harmful to the health or the development of the client or that may require excessive motivating operations to be in place" (BACB, 2014, p. 13). When we are talking about harmful reinforcers, we could be talking about things like cigarettes, nicotine, caffeine, sugar, or fat-laden foods, such as is possible when using edible reinforcers. This expectation does not mean we will never use any of these potential reinforcers; rather, we have an ethical obligation to ensure we are minimizing the use of them and that we are using them only when the need exists. In attempts to provide effective treatment across multiple domains, many providers and practitioners are responsible for influencing a great many decisions in the lives of their clients (Bannerman et al., 1990). As behavior analysts, we carry a large responsibility to include consumers in the planning of their treatment programs. For consumers who do not have the legal authority to consent, we must still aim to seek assent from the individual. Assent can look like allowing a technician to physically prompt a toothbrushing routine or jumping up to run to circle time when told it is time. When we identify a particular skill to observe, measure, or teach, we often can become hyper-focused on each and every occurrence of that behavior and may lose sight of the fact that people and their behaviors fluctuate and are unique to the individual. In their 1990 article "Balancing the Right to Habilitation with the Right to Personal Liberties: The Rights of People with Developmental Disabilities to Eat Too Many Doughnuts and Take a Nap," Bannerman and colleagues remind us of the importance of consumers' rights to habilitation and the freedom to choose, along with the potential difficulties associated with balancing the two. They focus on the need to ensure that we are teaching clients to make choices—choices that may increase a client's willingness to participate in activities that lead to greater habilitation.

The second right outlined by Van Houten and colleagues is that individuals have the right to services "with an overriding goal of personal welfare," which means the benefit must be for the client or the individual and those around them (1998, p. 382). The main purpose of behavioral treatment is to support individuals in acquiring skills that are functional and place an emphasis on promoting independence. We want to make sure that we are encouraging our clients to develop and demonstrate these skills, without ongoing support. When thinking about those who we work with, children will inevitably become teenagers, teenagers will become adults, and adults will become the elderly. We want to make sure we are considering immediate and long-term welfare when conducting assessments and developing interventions. Peer review and human rights committees have an important part in ensuring that adequate, effective, and unharmful interventions are available to our clients. In cases that involve potential risk, a peer review committee may play a distinct role in protecting the client's welfare. In contrast, a human rights committee is made up of consumers, advocates, and others in the community who use community standards to determine the social significance of our programs. For example, when living and working in warm climates, such as Hawaii, teaching individuals to put on their shoes and tie their shoelaces before they can go certain places may not be part of the community standard—particularly in cases where flip-flops, "slippahs," and sandals would be appropriate. Hence, there would be a low likelihood that the community would see shoe tying as a socially significant goal.

The third right described in the 1988 Van Houten et al. article is the "right to treatment by a competent behavior analyst" (p. 382). The definition of a competent behavior analyst is a professional who is responsible for delivering, directing, or evaluating treatment and has the education, training, and experience to do so. Competence in the clinical sphere requires robust and meaningful practicum training and supervision experiences.

Callout 16:

You are working as an analyst for a company that determines which clients to assign to you. Your agency informs you of a new client whose needs you feel are outside your scope of competence. You push back and let your supervisor know of your discomfort. In response, your supervisor tells you that you are the only analyst who has availability to take on this client. If you are unable to add this client to your caseload, your supervisor tells you the client will be unable to access care. What should you do? Use the three questions posed by Freeman, LeBlanc, and Martinez-Diaz (2020) to guide your answer.

The fourth right outlined in the article is the right to programs that teach functional skills. Our clients will need and will use functional skills, which will open their world to potentially new reinforcers. The goal for services is to increase the availability for individuals to access reinforcement as it occurs in the natural environment. It is not common for others to be walking around with tokens and delivering them contingent on a particular response in the natural environment. However, when you hold a door open for someone, often they will say thank you or will hold the door for you. That may be a reinforcer, if it increases your behavior in the future, and it occurs naturally in our everyday environments. Learning to talk, learning to read, and learning to drive open many, many more doors for us. We want to make sure the functional skills we teach our clients are pivotal skills, meaning they will open a whole world for them, providing access to a plethora of reinforcers in those natural environments.

As analysts, we seek to teach skills or behaviors that allow our clients to reduce unpleasant situations. For most of us, if there is something we want to avoid, we walk away from it or shut the door. We want to make sure we are encouraging and promoting this level of independence for our clients as well. When we talk about programs, which teach functional skills, we want to ensure that we are also eliminating behaviors that are dangerous or may be barriers to success. Every individual must have the right to access services that allow them to develop skills, which benefit not only themselves but also the community in which they live.

The fifth right is an individual's "right to a behavioral assessment and ongoing evaluation" (Van Houten et al., 1988, p. 383). Prior to services beginning, an individual should have an assessment that is comprehensive and complete. This process includes a functional analysis or functional behavior assessment, which emphasizes the importance of antecedent and consequences in the environment surrounding the behavior. An initial assessment must include the following: an interview and records review, direct observations, and the development of a treatment plan. Interviews will involve asking questions and determining circumstances, such as when does the behavior always occur? When does it never occur? When is it more likely to occur? What could you do to make the behavior occur right now? What do you do to make the behavior stop? When conducting direct observations, we are going to do so under varied and relevant circumstances. It is not necessarily helpful to observe a client only in a situation where others do not report that challenging behaviors occur. Common practice often involves conducting multiple observations and refraining from basing treatment plans solely on the reports of respondents from interviews and indirect assessments. We must ensure we are looking at various situations so we can see what success looks like, as well as what lack of success looks like, and so we can adequately describe the topography of challenging behavior for our clients. Finally, we must incorporate assessment findings and use this to guide the systematic development of appropriate treatment plans. Our plans must be written, and everyone who is responsible for implementing the plan must receive training on the implementation of each goal or program. Ongoing evaluation is crucial and is as important as conducting initial assessments. The initial assessment offers guidance for where to begin, and we must evaluate where we go from there on an ongoing basis. We want to ensure that our assessments include reviewing objective data and that we are looking at the effects of our treatments, as well as identifying any anticipated challenges. There are times when an outcome will occur that we did not—or could not—anticipate, even with appropriate protections in place. Looking at data that is visually displayed, on at least a biweekly basis, should help us mitigate or reduce challenges associated with our interventions. If the data suggest we need to make a change, then we must do so by modifying our treatment plans. As analysts, we are responsible for making these changes in a timely manner (BACB, 2020, 2.02). To be most effective, we must share the data and analysis regularly and directly with all members of the client's treatment team, including the client.

The sixth and final right mentioned in Van Houten et al.'s article is an individual's "right to the most effective treatment procedures available" (1988, p. 383). Our clients deserve and have an entitlement to efficacious and scientifically validated treatment. As a field, we are constantly striving to improve our practices. As our field grows, the need for our services continues to grow. Although it can be tempting to share an emerging trend with a client and the client's family, we must also make sure we are recommending only the interventions that have established scientific support. Effective treatment will require frequent data review, as discussed above, and the changes necessary to ensure client progress.

When we are providing services for our clients, we must delicately balance advocating for what they need with doing so within the parameters imposed by funding sources, which often include health insurers and school districts. Before 2001, most individuals who accessed behavior analytic services were required to pay out of pocket for care, restricting therapy to those who could afford it. Owing to substantial advocacy efforts, led primarily by caregivers of children with autism, health plans began providing meaningful coverage for ABA services in Indiana in 2001. It would be another 18 years before all 50 US states offered access to behavior analytic services, although most states limit this access to children or individuals with autism. In a Behaviorbabe podcast episode, Lorri Unumb, award-winning author, advocate, attorney, and autism parent, provides her perspectives on autism insurance and adult services (Kelly, 2019). Unumb details the decades-long advocacy efforts and takes a look at the challenges that lie ahead.

While health plans have provided access to services for many clients, this also presents additional areas for consideration, particularly as it relates to the role of third parties in the delivery of ABA services. As behavior analysts, we must be diligent and take the steps necessary to maintain the confidentiality of our clients and relevant stakeholders (BACB, 2020). We are expected to prevent the accidental dissemination of information and to remain in compliance with all confidentiality requirements set forth by BACB, state licensure boards, company policies, and laws. Confidentiality extends to information, whether we disseminate it synchronously, asynchronously, remotely, or in person, and it includes data and documentation, whether verbal, electronic, or written (BACB, 2020, 2.03).

Callout Box 17:

You send an email that includes some sensitive information to your supervisor about a shared client. However, instead of sending the email to your supervisor, you accidently send the email to a professor who has the same name. You have accidently shared confidential and sensitive client data with an unintended recipient. What steps do you take to immediately minimize and mitigate the risk of harm to your client?

Even when a violation is accidental or unintentional, it can still present significant harm to the client. In this case, our Ethics Code instructs us to take immediate and swift action to put the appropriate protections in place. In Scenario 17, an ethical violation has occurred. In addition to an ethical faux pas, this (unintentional) sharing of client information also presents a legal violation. The first step would be to contact your professor, share that the information received was intended for another recipient, and request deletion of the confidential information. We must also take appropriate steps to protect our agency by alerting our supervisor and compliance officer, if applicable. We must also inform the client what information was shared, as well as the steps we took to mitigate damage and reduce the risk of this occurring again.

Now imagine you are the recipient of an email containing confidential information. When you receive the message, what steps must you take? Naturally, you must alert the sender (your student) that you received information that was clearly intended for another recipient. You must also delete the email and refrain from referencing the contents of the email to others. This experience is a valuable, teachable moment. It is imperative that we do not presume our students' workplace will hold them to the same standards that we do, or that our students took the appropriate steps to notify their agency supervisor. Take this opportunity to speak to your student about the importance of protecting sensitive client information. You may wish to suggest use of a disclaimer at the end of each email, such as the following:

> This e-mail transmission (and/or the attachments accompanying it) may contain confidential information. This information is intended for use by the individual or entity named on this transmission. If you are not the intended recipient, you are hereby notified that any disclosure, copying, or distribution of any information in this transmission, or the taking of any action in reliance on the contents of this transmission, is strictly prohibited. Any unauthorized interception of this transmission is illegal under the law. If you have received this transmission in error, please promptly notify the sender by reply email and destroy all copies of this transmission.

When sharing client information with others, we must first ensure that we have obtained informed consent. The behavior analyst must get it from the client or the legal guardian for each person or organization the analyst wishes to contact, except in rare cases. Cases where the analyst may divulge information without first obtaining informed consent include situations in which the analyst is "attempting to protect the client or others from harm" or when a law or court order exists that compels the analyst to produce documents or to speak at a hearing (BACB, 2020, 2.04). When we receive authorization to release confidential information, we share only the information that is essential for the specified reason for the communication.

To comply with relevant laws, policies, ethics, and practices around maintaining confidentiality, one must be familiar with those laws, policies, and practices. From Roman law we follow the legal principle that ignorance of law excuses no one. This means that even if an individual has no knowledge of the law, they are still liable if they break that law (Holmes, 1991). The best protection we can afford our clients and ourselves begins with being knowledgeable about their rights and protections (BACB, 2020, 2.05). As behavior analysts, we are expected to maintain all client records for a period, and we refrain from destroying original records until the information is available in another way and/or the time frame required by law has passed. When we transition to a new organization, the responsibility for storing and maintaining records becomes the responsibility of the original organization and not the analyst.

Callout Box 18:

You have been working with a client for 3 years at your current agency. Legally, you realize you must store records and maintain them for a period of 7 years. Two years after you and your organization discharge the client from care, you leave your current agency. You take a copy of the client records with you in case the funding source makes a request for information. Which ethical code elements have you violated? What is the risk of harm to the client? What should you do instead to protect yourself, your former client, and the organization?

As behavior analysts, we have an obligation to accurately identify our services and to include all "required information on reports, bills, invoices, requests for reimbursement, and receipts" (BACB, 2020, 2.06), particularly with funding sources. Failure to do so not only constitutes an ethical but also a legal violation, which may have significant penalties attached. In most situations, practitioners do not intentionally engage in unethical and illegal billing practices; however, there are numerous opportunities for unintentional violations, which remain violations nonetheless and present a significant risk of harm to the clients we serve.

Callout Box 19:

You are working with a 25-year-old adult, who has a diagnosis of ADHD and health plan approval to receive behavior analytic services. The client wants to learn how to swim, and you agree that you can dedicate a portion of the session to teaching this skill. While learning to swim is an important life skill, you realize you do not have any goals in your treatment plan that are appropriate to teach at a community pool. In your session note, instead of listing the community as the location, you list the client's home. After all, you *did* start the session in the client's home. Is this decision ethical? Is it legal? What is the potential of harm to the client? What is the right thing to do?

It is critical as analysts that we are familiar with, and frequently reference, our Ethics Code. As previously discussed, there are numerous instances when a solution to a situation may not be apparent. However, there are certain situations in which the Code speaks clearly to us, such as in Scenario 19.

When we are operating under a contract specifically for behavioral services, code 2.06 Accuracy in Service Billing and Reporting clarifies that, behavior analysts do not provide services or charge for them if they are non behavioral in nature (BACB, 2020). When we uncover inaccuracies in billing or reporting, the Code notes that we must immediately inform all relevant parties, take steps to correct the error in a timely manner, and document the steps taken as well as the ultimate outcomes.

As mentioned, steadfast advocacy from unrelenting caregivers of children with autism has led to the passage of meaningful autism insurance reform (and access to behavior analytic services) in all 50 US states. Health plans have assessed and determined a range of reimbursement for a menu of services that behavior analysts provide. However, actual reimbursement rates vary depending on each agency or analyst's specific agreement with each funding source. As behavior analysts, we have an ethical obligation to implement billing practices and share billing information in accordance with relevant rules and regulations, which are set forth by funding sources, federal and state laws, and regulatory boards and agencies. Furthermore, we must not misrepresent our fees, bill for services we did not provide or have an authorization to provide, or ask families to offset the cost if we have negotiated too low a rate with health plans (BACB, 2020, 2.07). Behavior analysts and the services we provide are also subject to antitrust laws, which governments develop to ensure consumer protection from predatory business practices. Put differently, it is illegal for behavior analysts to discuss rates with other providers, to set rate expectations across the field, or to hold insurance companies to a predetermined, fieldwide minimum or maximum hourly fee. The exception to this is with publicly available rates, such as with the federal Medicaid program or with TRICARE, which provides support for military beneficiaries. Antitrust laws exist to protect consumers against price fixing, price discrimination, and monopolization.

As behavior analysts, we are expected to communicate about our services with clients *before* initiating services. When doing so, we must "use understandable language" with "stakeholders, supervisees, trainees, and research participants" (BACB, 2020, 2.08). Pat Friman, a psychologist with specific training in the science of behavior analysis, has been a long-time advocate encouraging behavior analysts to use consumer-friendly language in our communications with families, as well in our dissemination and advocacy efforts. If you are not yet familiar with the work of Pat Friman, we encourage you to do more research into his contributions to our field and into the widespread adoption of behavior analytic concepts.

Science is the basis for everything we do, but speaking as scientists to caregivers, teachers, and other nonbehavior analysts prevents us from connecting with our audience, and it ultimately leads to misconceptions about behavior analysis. If we do not make the information about what we do accessible to the public, we will never fully see the concepts and benefits to society actualized. As analysts, we must communicate information about our services, the client's assessments and goals, and specific treatment protocols in language that is easy for stakeholders to understand. For example, when speaking with consumers, instead of referring to a client "manding" for specific items, you can note that they were "asking" or "requesting" to play with bubbles. The key component to communicate when discussing verbal behavior, specifically "mands," is for motivation to be present. We can communicate this concept without using specific behavioral jargon or terminology. Instead of noting that we are using "differential reinforcement to increase manding," we can say something like "We provide different responses when your child asks for bubbles. When they say 'bubbles' on their own, we blow bubbles for about 30 seconds. When we provide a prompt to say 'bubbles,' we only blow bubbles for about 3 seconds."

When selecting treatment goals and behaviors for increase and/or decrease, we must always consult and consider the preferences of the client and related stakeholders. To this end, as analysts, we must ensure that we include clients and stakeholders at the onset of assessment, during treatment, and during the service relationship (BACB, 2020, 2.09). We must consult with our clients when identifying goals, selecting assessment tools to use, and designing treatment protocols. Furthermore, the expectation is that this practice should be ongoing, rather than something we do only at the onset of a provider-client relationship. Behavior analysts are responsible for ensuring that we conduct ongoing progress monitoring and that we are checking in with our clients continually throughout the duration of the relationship.

Being a behavior analyst can be a daunting and overwhelming career choice. There is the expectation that we balance our client's needs with restrictions imposed by funding sources. We are challenged to balance the preferences of caregivers with prioritizing the needs and preferences of the client. We are responsible for supervising technicians and collaborating with medical and educational teams (BACB, 2020, 2.10).

In addition to these responsibilities, we must obtain continuing education and engage in frequent professional development activities, all the while trying to achieve the ever-elusive life-work balance. What we do is hard work—there is no doubt about that. We are constantly striving to better ourselves and to better support our clients in meeting their goals. In addition to involving our clients in their programming, we must collaborate with other individuals who have expertise in areas we do not. This collaboration can range from working as part of an interdisciplinary team at a hospital, clinic, or school to reaching out to colleagues in our field who may have additional experience or an expanded scope of competence.

Owing to several factors within and beyond our control, conflicts can occur when collaborating. A common barrier to collaboration is that we often have different information and interpretations about the same event. Our interpretations come from different life experiences that have shaped the lens through which we see the world. When disagreements occur, we may find ourselves reacting emotionally. When we are in a difficult situation, we often assume we know the intentions of the other person. Our assumptions are often wrong because we base them on our own feelings. If we are hurting, we believe the other party was intending to hurt us, which is often not the case.

One way to better understand another person's intentions is to ask them. However, a lack of administrative approval for planning meetings—more than disagreements about treatment—is the most frequently cited barrier to collaboration in workplace settings (Nochajski, 2002). This challenge is more compounded in our field, as many insurance-funded services do not provide reimbursement for collaboration with other professionals. Some agencies restrict the amount of time analysts may interact with other professionals, which limits the possibility of effective collaboration, especially if this collaboration is nonbillable.

Collaboration is critical for achieving the best client outcomes possible. It is important to know how to navigate difficult conversations, which means acknowledging how our own behavior may be making matters worse. Obviously, approaching a situation with the assumption that the other person has nothing to contribute is not going to yield positive outcomes. Other ways we may alienate others is by using precise terms and definitions and aptly correcting anyone who uses these terms differently than we do. In 1953, B. F. Skinner noted,

> Verbal behavior is successful only when it generates suitable behavior in the average listener; therefore, the form of the behavior comes to correspond more and more closely to the standards of a given community. When we move from one community to another, the topography of our behavior may change (p. 97).

It is important to speak with precision in professional presentations and publications, but we must adapt our behavior by adopting language that is understandable to our current communication partners. In an article published by Richard Foxx (1996), he called on behavior analysts to be behavioral ambassadors and translators, noting:

> Behavioral ambassadors and translators speak many languages and are sensitive to how others react to and interpret what is being said. They always consider their listeners' learning history and talk to them in their own language or model. They evaluate what they are intending to say and the impact it might have on the listener before they speak. Their goal is to effectively translate the behavior-analytical model to others (p. 154).

As behavior analysts, we have the challenge of extending competence while tempering arrogance or overconfidence. We must speak with precision, yet also with flexibility and fluency with various audiences. We must be professional, yet personable, while diligent to avoid conflicts and dual relationships. In true collaborative fashion, let us lean on experts in other professions for tips on how to become effective communicators. In "Difficult Conversations: How to Discuss What Matters Most," from the Harvard Negotiation Project, authors Stone, Patton, and Heen (2010) provide strategies for how to start conversations without putting others on the defensive, suggesting we begin by using "I" statements—for example, "I hear what you are saying" or "I do not completely understand." If you agree with part of the point another person is making, you can use this to build common ground: "I agree with you on X, and I think we could explore a few alternate ideas as well." When we are brainstorming with others, it can become easy to focus on sharing our ideas, rather than first pausing to hear the ideas of others. To be effective communication partners, these authors urge us to learn to listen, suggesting we seek first to understand and then to be understood.

Naturally, before any consultation or collaboration with other professionals can occur, we must know and comply with confidentiality and consent requirements for communicating with third parties. Behavior analysts, like many other medical and educational professionals, are expected to explain assessment and treatment procedures before obtaining consent from clients and relevant stakeholders. What's more, behavior analysts must document all efforts we make, in writing, when obtaining informed consent (BACB, 2020, 2.11). When applicable (which we would suggest is always), we are also responsible for obtaining *assent* from clients. The BACB Ethics Code defines assent as "vocal or nonvocal verbal behavior that can be taken to indicate willingness to participate in research or behavioral services by individuals who cannot provide informed consent (e.g., because of age or intellectual impairments)" (BACB, 2020, p. 7).

Callout Box 20:

You are providing support to a 9-year-old child and his family in their home. When conducting your interview, you ask about priorities for goals to address. The client and his mother provide you with a list of four behaviors they want to tackle with your support. The list includes learning to tie shoes, reducing aggressive behaviors, learning to ride a bike, and decreasing swearing behavior toward caregivers and younger siblings. How do you prioritize which behaviors to teach first? First, you are off to a great start by including the client as well as his mother in the discussion. Next, consider separating the client and his mother (e.g., one is on the couch in the living room and the other is at the kitchen table) and asking them to rank-order the four behavioral targets from most to least important.

When prioritizing targets, as in Scenario 20, we must resist the urge to immediately default to sharing our own thoughts and opinions on how we would prioritize them. At this moment, we have the opportunity to listen and learn from the client and caregiver. Once they share their ideas with us, it is up to us to guide the discussion and to share our recommendations with them, pausing again once we do to ask and evaluate if the plan we are proposing is acceptable to all parties involved.

As behavior analysts, we are expected to recommend and obtain medical clearance before treating behaviors, particularly those that are likely to have a medical cause. By ensuring that we have obtained consent for collaboration with other medical professionals at the onset of client care, we are setting the stage for ensuring ongoing consultation with medical professionals (BACB, 2020, 2.12).

Callout Box 21:

You receive a request to consult with a 16-year-old and their caregivers. One of the behaviors of concern includes urinary accidents or "leaks." Before developing a behavior intervention plan, you recommend that the client receive clearance from a urologist. The family is a little bit hesitant; however, you remain firm and let them know you will develop an intervention once they receive clearance from a qualified physician. The family eventually schedules the appointment with the urologist. After the evaluation, the determination is made that the client has a defective bladder, which is contributing to the urinary accidents. Based on this information, you develop an intervention plan focusing on wearing, checking, and changing pantyliners and scheduling bathroom breaks, especially during highly preferred activities. How might you design the intervention plan differently without this medical consideration? Is it ethical to hold the client accountable for something that is not in their control? What might be the harm in doing so? This scenario is only one example that emphasizes the importance of seeking medical clearance, especially when treating complicated and complex behaviors.

Whenever making medical referrals, it is important to document these conversations. Many agencies have policies for documenting phone calls, caregiver sessions, and medical consultations. This documentation can be as simple as a handwritten note that you place in a client's physical record or an electronic record stored in an online platform.

As behavior analysts, we place an emphasis on maximizing benefits and limiting potential for harm for our clients and stakeholders when choosing, designing, and delivering assessments (BACB, 2020, 2.13). By doing so we are selecting assessments that are relevant to the age and profile of the learner. It also means we individualize the assessment and provide recommendations for treatment, which are best practices and the most relevant for our client.

Callout Box 22:

You are conducting an initial assessment for a client who is 25 years old and described as being fully verbal. You have not worked with a client with this profile before. Typically, you work with early learners who are developing language, and for those clients you often select the Verbal Behavior Milestones Assessment and Placement Program (VB-MAPP), and generally you select the next three goals per domain in the same order as they appear on the assessment tool. You realize this assessment will not be acceptable for your incoming client, so you consult with your supervisor, who has more experience than you with older clients. She offers to train you in other assessments, such as the Essential for Living (EFL) and the Assessment of Functional Living Skills (AFLS), to co-conduct the assessment, and to assist with writing the treatment plan. Do these adjustments resolve all ethical concerns described in this scenario?

Referencing the scenario related to assessments (Scenario 22), there is one piece of information that presents as potentially concerning: *You often select the VB-MAPP and generally select the next three goals per domain in the same order as they appear on the assessment tool.* This decision is concerning for a number of reasons. Let us walk through the Ethics Code and consider which elements might pertain to this scenario: 1.05 Practicing within Scope of Competence, 2.01 Providing Effective Treatment, and 2.13 Selecting, Designing, and Implementing Assessments seem potentially applicable. The problem with prescribing treatment goals directly in order as they appear on an assessment tool is that they may not take into consideration other skill deficits or needs or cultural considerations. This rigidity in selecting treatment goals can lead to cookie-cutter programming that is not individualized and therefore does not maximize the outcomes for the client. This decision also suggests that perhaps the analyst has an underdeveloped repertoire when it comes to conceptualizing programming for clients. This—that is, having an underdeveloped skillset—is natural and okay and has occurred for all of us at one time or another. An underdeveloped skillset is an opportunity to learn more and grow as analysts. It is not possible to digest and synthesize everything in the field in the few years it will take to complete a degree and coursework. Analysts, both early-career and seasoned alike, are constantly learning skills, which is why it is so critical for us to maintain certification and seek professional development opportunities and continuing education events (see BACB, 2020, 1.05).

Another way behavior analysts and technicians reduce risk to clients is by recommending only evidenced-based procedures. This choice may seem like a no-brainer; however, nothing is as black or white as it may seem when it comes to ethics. For starters, how do we define evidence based? How connected are we with the current literature? How often do we return to the original resources? How fluent are we with the application of certain principles and procedures? Are we simply recommending what has worked for us or our clients in the past? It is easy to find ourselves getting caught up in the hustle and bustle of our day-to-day responsibilities. However, it is also our responsibility to stay current, to attend conferences, to establish and maintain relationships with mentors, and to immerse ourselves in the literature. When there is more than one acceptable course of action and a potential disagreement about which course to pursue, behavior analysts must consider the pros and cons, likelihood of dangerous side effects, preference of the client and stakeholders, efficacy of the treatments we select, and cost-effectiveness that we associate with the treatment (BACB, 2020, 2.14).

Ethically, behavior analysts must minimize risks associated with behavior change interventions (BACB, 2020, 2.15). When considering the risks, benefits, and side effects of our interventions, we must ensure that we are selecting interventions that will have the highest fidelity of implementation accuracy. This decision may mean selecting a slightly less effective procedure over a more effective procedure requiring extensive resources and additional training that are unavailable to current team members. This responsibility also means prioritizing positive procedures over more intrusive or punishment-based procedures, unless the potential for harm eclipses the risk associated with the intervention (2.15). Both punishment and penalty will stop existing behaviors. However, they will not teach new behaviors. Behavior, which we stop through punishment and penalty, will reoccur when we remove the threat of punishment or penalty (Daniels, 2009).

Callout Box 23:

You are supervising a child's programming and see during a group circle time with others that the child repeatedly stands up during times when the rest of the group is sitting on the floor. The teacher gives the instruction to sit down, yet the child does not sit. You then direct the technician to remove the child from the activity. The child leaves while crying, hitting, and kicking. This behavior continues upon arrival in the session room and the child starts to throw items from tables and cubbies. You direct the technician to remove the child from circle time in the future if not following instructions to sit with the group. What benefits does this intervention have? What risks does it have on the client? What can we do differently?

Pokorski and Barton (2020) review research studies containing punishment-based procedures and their effects on young children with disabilities, both in special education and in ABA practices. Their investigation explored the characteristics of participants and treatments and the degree to which ethical standards were adhered to by researchers. The results indicate that a variety of punishment-based procedures have been used and that these procedures generally result in decreased challenging behavior, which was demonstrated across age, diagnosis, behaviors, and treatment type. However, in this investigation, the ethics of these punishment-based interventions were called into question. Pokorski and Barton suggest an ethics code specific for research practices, as well as the development of tools to aid practitioners in recognizing ethical implications of selecting punishment-based interventions.

As discussed, when communicating with clients and stakeholders, we are expected to do so in a way that our clients can understand what we are saying (BACB, 2020, 2.16). Imagine if you went to a doctor who spoke to you in only technical terms. You will be not only confused but also frustrated with questions and no answers. Is this how you want your clients to feel when they interact with you or when reading your reports and recommendations? No, it is not. We want our clients to feel supported and excited about interacting with us. To do this, we must take the time and care to explain the results of our assessments and the components of our treatment plans in ways the client and related stakeholders can understand. Take, for example, the following sentence: "In response to the antecedents observed, it seems likely your child is engaging in attention-seeking behavior, which is being positively reinforced." How else might we communicate this same information in a less technical and less awkward manner? Perhaps we can say something like this: "I noticed that every time you are on the phone or speaking to someone at the store your son begins shouting and calling your name. When he does, you often end your conversation and give him your undivided attention. It is possible this response could be maintaining the behavior." Sure, it may take a few extra words or sentences to communicate the same information, but if your listener does not understand what you are saying, how effectively were you communicating in the first place?

One of the main tenets of behavior analysis is the reliance on objective decision making. Using data to guide decisions can help take the emotion out of the discussion, which is particularly useful when there is a difference of opinion. Take, for example, the story of Claire, a fourth-grade teacher, and a student who is standing on the desk during class and making a scene. When meeting with the behavior consultant, Claire suggested having the student earn time on the computer for classes during which he did not call out or stand on his desk. The consultant responded by stating that the student was engaging in the behavior to access Claire's attention and also was getting some attention for the behavior from peers. The consultant suggested a reinforcement system by which the student could earn access to Claire's attention. Claire was agreeable to this suggestion; however, she did not feel it was going to be effective. After considering what the consultant shared, Claire persisted and told the consultant she wanted to use the computer as the incentive. Rather than insist that Claire try her way, or throw her hands in the air in defeat and give in to Claire, the consultant suggested trying both. Claire and the consultant wrote down each condition on separate pieces of paper and put them in a coffee mug on Claire's desk. Every day for 15 days, or three school weeks, Claire pulled a slip and provided the corresponding reward (e.g., computer, attention). This procedure meant that sometimes the student could earn the computer two days in a row. Sometimes, two or three days in a row, the student earned time with Claire. The idea was to counterbalance the conditions in a pattern that no one could predict. At the end of the three school weeks, Claire and her consultant reviewed the data. They noted a reduction in challenging behavior across both conditions. What Claire also noticed by looking at the data was the steeper reduction in behavior when earning access to her attention. This experience provided Claire and her consultant the opportunity to revisit their discussion on function-based interventions. It also allowed the consultant to respect Claire's expertise and the fact that it was Claire's classroom. Claire implemented each condition with fidelity, perhaps because she wanted to prove her consultant wrong. And what if she had? What comes from this interaction is an appreciation for the information. With the data, Claire had the power to make an informed decision, with the consultant there only as a guide.

When communicating with clients and related stakeholders (e.g., caregivers, physicians, etc.), it is imperative for us to rely on data to form our impressions, rather than to rely on opinions or recollections. It is not enough simply to collect data; we must also visually display and analyze the data that we collect. Think back to the individuals you asked to collect data (e.g., Registered Behavior Technicians [RBTs], caregivers, teachers). How likely are they to continue collecting data if they do not see the value, if we are not connecting for them the power of visual analysis? With that said, we must take great care to present meaningful data displays and to use the data to help us paint a picture to tell the story.

Callout Box 24:

You work for an agency that uses an electronic data collection platform. When you start with the company, you are provided with training on the data collection system. When you go to input your programs, you notice the data collection tab defaults to displaying percentage data. You search until you find the appropriate dimension of measurement for the behavior of interest. You make a comment to your supervisor about how effortful it was to switch the dimension of measurement in the system, and you remark, "I wonder how many analysts end up selecting percent just because it's easier?" A few months later, a colleague transitions to a new position in the agency and you absorb some of that person's cases. When you do, you notice that for every behavior for each client, only percentage data are being collected, including when tracking tantrums and other behaviors, which are episodic in nature. You understand how this error happened but realize that the client's data displays are not painting an accurate picture. What would you do?

Let us assume in Scenario 24 that you made the appropriate changes and realize you need to update the client's programming, so you take the time to make those updates. It is important that as behavior analysts we are continually evaluating—and adjusting, when warranted—our behavior-change programs (BACB, 2020, 2.18). When data show that the client is not achieving the outcomes as intended, we have a commitment to identify and assess potential barriers and to take appropriate steps to remedy the situation, which in this scenario has been done. You may notice when you assume such cases that there are factors interfering with service delivery. When we find ourselves in such circumstances, it is our responsibility to remove barriers and minimize problematic situations, which are actions that increase variability in the data we collect, as well as in the outcomes we help our clients achieve. We can make modifications to treatment protocols when the data warrant a change; however, if we are unsure of what else we can modify, we must consider obtaining help from other experts and possibly referring to other professionals as well (2.19).

Section 2 of our Ethics Code involves maintaining our responsibilities to our profession. While the many tasks that behavior analysts do on a daily basis can make this challenging, we encourage you to think about what is in the best interest of the client. This process includes involving clients and relevant stakeholders in discussions of assessments and appropriate treatment goals; gaining informed consent and the assent of our clients; taking, updating, and relying on data to make program changes; and collaborating with other relevant people in the client's life. When we make the client our first priority, we are able to better see how our use of appropriate assessments, programming for natural reinforcers, keeping long-term and immediate effects of our programming in mind, and including the client in program decisions will impact the life of the client for the better.

References

Bannerman, D. J., Sheldon, J. B., Sherman, J. A., & Harchik, A. E. (1990). Balancing the right to habilitation with the right to personal liberties: The rights of people with developmental disabilities to eat too many doughnuts and take a nap. *Journal of Applied Behavior Analysis, 23*(1), 79−89. https://doi.org/10.1901/jaba.1990.23-79

Behavior Analyst Certification Board (BACB). (2014). *Professional and ethical compliance code for behavior analysts.* Author.

Behavior Analyst Certification Board (BACB). (2020). Ethics code for behavior analysts. https://bacb.com/wp-content/ethics-code-for-behavior-analysts.

Daniels, A. C. (2009). *Oops! 13 management practices that waste time and money (and what to do instead).* Performance Management Publications.

Foxx, R. M. (1996). Translating the covenant: The behavior analyst as ambassador and translator. *The Behavior Analyst, 19*(2), 147−161. https://doi.org/10.1007/bf03393162

Freeman, T., LeBlanc, L., & Martinez-Diaz, J. (2020). Ethical and professional responsibilities of applied behavior analysts. In J. Cooper, T. Heron, & W. Heward (Eds.), *Applied behavior analysis* (3rd ed., pp. 757−782). essay, Pearson Education.

Holmes, O. W., & Novick, S. M. (1991). *The common law.* Dover Publications.

Kelly, A. N. (2019). *Lorri unumb on autism insurance and adult services (Audio podcast episode).* Behaviorbabe. https://anchor.fm/behaviorbabe/episodes/Lorri-Unumb-on-Autism-Insurance-and-Adult-Services-e3a3et.

Nochajski, S. M. (2002). Collaboration between team members in inclusive educational settings. *Occupational Therapy in Health Care, 15*(3−4), 101−112. https://doi.org/10.1080/j003v15n03_06

Pokorski, E. A., & Barton, E. E. (2020). A systematic review of the ethics of punishment-based procedures for young children with disabilities. *Remedial and Special Education, 42*(4), 262−275. https://doi.org/10.1177/0741932520918859

Skinner, B. F. (1953). *Science and human behavior.* Free Press.

Stone, D., Patton, B., & Heen, S. (2010). *Difficult conversations: How to discuss what matters most.* Portfolio/Penguin.

Van Houten, R., Axelrod, S., Bailey, J. S., Favell, J. E., Foxx, R. M., Iwata, B. A., & Lovaas, O. I. (1988). The right to effective behavioral treatment. *Journal of Applied Behavior Analysis, 21*(4), 381−384. https://doi.org/10.1901/jaba.1988.21-381

Discussion questions

1. What are the six rights of clients regarding effective behavioral treatment?
2. Why might you teach clients to expand their repertoire of preferred activities (e.g., songs)?
3. What steps might a behavior analyst take to decrease the likelihood of distress for clients?
4. What are some considerations behavior analysts must take into account when deciding whether or not to use edible reinforcers?
5. Why is it important to consider immediate and long-term welfare when conducting assessments and developing interventions?
6. What is the significance of the physical environment when selecting which skills to teach to clients in a particular community?
7. How do the authors describe a competent behavior analyst? What would you add or change about this definition?
8. What is the benefit to observing clients in more than one setting when conducting assessments or developing programs?
9. How long did it take for autism insurance mandates to be enacted in all 50 US states? What are some limitations of current laws or practices?
10. What are antitrust laws, and what do they aim to protect consumers against?

Section 3

Responsibility to clients and stakeholders

"The first step in the evolution of ethics is a sense of solidarity with other human beings."

Albert Schweitzer

Discussion questions
1. Why is it critical for behavior analysts to use understandable language when communicating with clients and relevant stakeholders?
2. Behavior analysts are expected to juggle multiple tasks and responsibilities. List five common expectations of behavior analysts.
3. What is assent? How does it differ from consent? Why is it important to obtain both assent and consent?

Section 3 of our Ethics Code focuses on our responsibilities to our clients and other stakeholders. Again, it is through a lens of keeping our client's best interests at heart that we delve into this section of the code. Section 3 focuses

Back to Basics. https://doi.org/10.1016/B978-0-323-85566-2.00004-3

on how we accept clients, identify and work with relevant stakeholders, maintain confidentiality, appropriately document our services, and advocate for any other necessary services for our clients. In addition, we will discuss how to ethically terminate your relationship with a client and stakeholders, either because the client is no longer in need of services or because you are transitioning them to another provider.

As behavior analysts, the work we do is most impactful to our clients. Ultimately, the services we provide to our clients should benefit them and present no harm. We must help support our client's rights (BACB, 2020, 3.01) by first identifying who the client is and then the relevant stakeholders involved (3.02). As behavior analysts, we must protect the best interest of the client, who the BACB defines as "the direct recipient of [our] services" (p. 3). In some cases, the client may be the only individual involved, which can be the case when working with adults. Often, we involve caregivers as well as other stakeholders such as health plans, school districts, or other third parties. At differing times during the service relationship, one or more related parties may meet the definition of a client concurrently—for example, when they are receiving consultation or training from the behavior analyst. In certain situations the definition of *client* also extends to groups of individuals, as when providing organizational consultation.

Callout Box 25:

A child's grandparents contact you to start services for their grandchild. First, you may need to ask if they are custodial guardians for this child, or you may need to gather more information on the child's legal situation. If the grandparents are indeed custodial guardians, additional paperwork is necessary to demonstrate this legal relationship and ensure that you establish services with the stakeholder who has legal and medical decision-making rights for this child. If the grandparents are not the legal guardians but are helping the child's legal guardian by gathering information, you can tell them about your ABA services so that they can take the information back to the family. Could you directly contact the grandchild's legal guardian with only an inquiry from the grandparents? What ethical codes may impact this situation?

Behavior analysts may face another situation in which clients turn age 18 during services or are new clients over the age of 18. If a caregiver contacts you for services for their 20-year-old child, pause and ask yourself these questions: Who is the client? Is there any type of legal guardianship established for the caregivers? Does the client want services?

Callout Box 26:

You have a client who turns 18 while actively receiving services with you. In the eyes of the government, the client becomes an adult. Caregivers may face difficult and lengthy paths in their state to establish guardianship if their child is unable to

---

Callout Box 26:—cont'd

make medical and legal decisions for themselves. If the caregivers have legal guardianship, paperwork should be in the client's files. If caregivers have not yet obtained guardianship or do not need to do so, the client is now responsible for giving consent, in addition to assent for services received. Additional paperwork must now go directly to the client. The client will be responsible for signing any documents, such as treatment plans and consent for services. What should you do if the client does not want to continue services? What can we, as behavior analysts do, in situations such as these? We can explain the services that we have been providing and the current recommendation for services. We can advocate for continuing services until the client attains certain benchmark skills. Hopefully, we are involving our client in the decision-making process regarding treatment before they turn 18 and the client understands and agrees with the goals of treatment. Ultimately, the client in this situation has full power and rights to continue or stop services. We must support the client's rights even when we do not agree.

When new clients are coming into our care, we must do an initial case review and ask ourselves a few questions: Does this client's needs fit into my scope of competence? Do I have the supervisory capacity to take on another client? Have I identified a technician who can work with this client? If the answer to any of these is no, we must do additional investigation before providing services to the client (BACB, 2020, 3.03). These situations put analysts in tricky situations. An analyst may need more training on a specific topic before taking the client or may need to find a mentor who can be more intimately involved in treatment planning. If this is not possible, it may be necessary to refer the client to a different service provider. Analysts may find themselves uncomfortable about needing to tell their supervisors that they cannot accept a client due to lack of training, capacity, or staffing, which can be daunting and incredibly challenging to do. Ultimately, however, more harm could come to the client if the analyst accepts a client outside their scope of competence and available resources.

Callout Box 27:

You are a brand-new, recently certified analyst. Your fieldwork and experience consist of children with autism, ages 2 to 7. You start at a new company and take over an existing caseload. While reviewing your clients, you see that one client is a 17-year-old who exhibits aggressive behaviors, including shoving, choking, hitting, punching, and kicking. Due to current staffing issues, the client is only receiving services for 10 out of 20 recommended hours. What is your ethical obligation regarding advocating for an appropriate service density? What steps should you take? How can you resolve this dilemma so that you follow the BACB Ethics Code, while allowing the client to receive effective services?

There are many areas in the field of behavior analysis: autism, organizational behavior management, sports, behavioral gerontology, traumatic brain injury, and substance abuse, to name a few. It is impossible for behavior analysts to specialize and develop expertise in all areas of potential application. Consider the following: A company that focuses on organizational behavioral management (OBM) approaches an analyst who has experience working exclusively in the field of autism. How might the analyst respond ethically? Think of the core principles when examining this scenario.

We establish service agreements at the start of services between the analyst/organization and the client and/or stakeholders (BACB, 2020, 3.04). This agreement outlines the behavior analytic services that we will provide, explains responsibilities of all parties, and includes information about the ethics code that all analysts must follow. Contact must also include information on how to report complaints about the analyst. This process includes submitting complaints to the BACB, the analyst's organization; any applicable licensing organization such as state boards; and funders. If we need to update services agreements, we must have all parties review and resign them.

Before embarking into a relationship for a client on the behalf of a third party, such as a health plan or school district, we must obtain written consent from the client or relevant stakeholder (e.g., legal guardian) (BACB, 2020, 3.09). You may be surprised how many times this situation comes up over a behavior analyst's career.

> **Callout Box 28:**
>
> You work in a public school district. Your supervisor, the special education director for the district, contacts you by email requesting a functional behavior assessment (FBA) for a third-grade student. You respond via email that you can begin immediately. You ask for a copy of the student's IEP and written consent from the caregivers. Your supervisor informs you that the IEP and consent forms will be forthcoming. You reply to your supervisor that you will get started as soon as you receive the consent. She replies, "FBAs do not require consent," and instructs you to start the assessment the following day. You may find yourself having to make a very uncomfortable choice. Do you upset your supervisor, or do you engage in a potential ethical violation?

When we think of the three guiding questions posed by Freeman, LeBlanc, and Martinez-Diaz (2020), we immediately remember that it is our clients' interests that we are looking to protect. In Scenario 28, we can ask ourselves three guiding questions: (1) "What is the right thing to do?" The potential of harm is immense. We should not evaluate the client and make determinations without first obtaining the written consent of the caregiver. (2) "What is worth doing?" The right thing would be to hold off on conducting the assessment until you receive written consent. You may wish to offer to reach out to the family directly to obtain the consent for the assessment. (3) "What does it mean to be a 'good' behavior analyst?" In this case, a behavior analyst who is behaving ethically is someone who has obtained consent, as well as assent, from the client when possible.

Discussing payment before providing services is another way to eliminate confusion and to create clarity around provider-client relationships, particularly those that a third-party arranges (BACB, 2020, 3.05). Decades ago, when analysts were first trained and practicing, there was no insurance funding for ABA services, which explains their omission from course syllabi. ABA services have become more popular, and as of 2019, nearly two decades after the formation of the BACB, all 50 US states provide insurance coverage of ABA for individuals with autism. This new funding source has resulted in many analysts jumping into the role of healthcare provider without the necessary background and training to understand medical necessity, healthcare funder guidelines and requirements, and how to ensure our documentation meets those requirements. What are our ethical obligations regarding our understanding of insurance-funded ABA services? How can we ensure that we are making appropriate recommendations in light of funding source guidelines and restrictions?

There must be contracts and financial agreements in place prior to starting services (BACB, 2020, 3.05, 3.07). This expectation delineates the responsibilities of the parties and sets expectations, including limits pertaining to maintaining confidentiality (3.07). Limits to confidentiality may also be set by law and include mandated reporting of suspected child abuse and neglect. We must inform all parties involved in services of limits pertaining to confidentiality, including the client, legal guardians, and possible third parties (3.10). Other times, a behavior analyst may need to discuss a client with another provider to ensure that they are working in the best interest of the client. To discuss a client with another provider we must obtain informed consent. Situations warranting this may include additional consultation or making referrals to another provider. An analyst may not discuss a client without informed consent from the client or responsible stakeholder (3.06).

Even when working through a third-party contractor, analysts must put the needs of the client above everything else (BACB, 2020, 3.08). If asked to perform work outside the scope of behavior analysis, an analyst must work to resolve this conflict, as it could have a negative impact on the client. When a third party hires an analyst to work with a child or adult who has a legal guardian, the analyst must ensure that the legal caregiver or guardian is included in service decisions. Involving caregivers means explaining to them the services you will provide and their rights within them. Caregivers and legal guardians also have the right to access and obtain all documentation of services, even when you provide services through a third party (3.09). For example, if a school establishes a contract for a student to receive ABA services during school days, caregivers must be a part of the process of establishing care. Caregivers can also have access to all treatment plans and session notes and may attend meetings related to behavior analytic service delivery for their child, even though sessions do not take place outside of the school building.

Working with insurance funders adds a layer of complexity to the services we provide. Insurance companies maintain their own medical necessity criteria, which may stray from what is best for the client and what are the best practices in the field of behavior analysis. When there are disagreements between your medical recommendation and what the health plan authorizes, remember your ethical obligation to advocate for appropriate services for your clients (BACB, 2020, 3.12). Situations may arise where attempts are made to limit the number of service hours you recommend. Should you negotiate with the funding source? How do you effectively advocate for your client? In a 2018 podcast episode, Jennifer Lonardo, a behavior analyst who resides on the Island of Hawaii, joins the show to discuss strategies for effectively and ethically advocating for access to behavior analytic services, including across multiple treatment settings (Kelly, 2018). Lonardo provides valuable insight for analysts on how we can advocate through negotiation, without feeling as if we are compromising our ethics. As professionals, we need to advocate for what our client needs, not what the third-party contractor says it will fund.

Families also experience barriers to services. For many, there are simply not enough hours in the day. For some school-age children, schedules are packed with school, ABA therapy, speech therapy, occupational therapy, soccer, music lessons, and so on. What's more, most caregivers are also working and tending to other family members. With only 24 hours in a day and the need for homework, dinner, and bedtime, there is only so much one can juggle. The families we serve are facing incredibly difficult decisions about their children and their children's access to care. As behavior analysts, we must advocate for the appropriate service density for our clients to make meaningful outcomes (BACB, 2020, 3.12), while decreasing the stress and strain on the client and family unit whenever possible. In a 2019 podcast episode, Kate Disney, an autism parent advocate, who is also a military veteran, retired nurse, and behavior analyst, offers her unique perspective on what it looks like for military families to access ABA services (Kelly, 2019). Disney shares with listeners both the "unavoidable and avoidable aspects associated with transitions, moves, and deployments." Disney offers suggestions for caregivers and providers alike about what can be done to mitigate the effects of these transitions on the family unit.

Behavior analysts must document all behavior analytic work that they perform (BACB, 2020, 3.11). Various funding sources may require specific documentation for each session note, but the general content must reflect a subjective, objective, assessment, and plan (SOAP) note. Documentation maintains accountability in services, and various funding sources are likely to require this information. These documents can also be useful when collaborating with other medical and education providers and when transitioning services from one provider or agency to another.

Many of our clients may need services in addition to the services a behavior analyst can provide. We must base referrals to outside providers on what our clients need above what is convenient. When a referral to another provider is needed, behavior analysts must provide multiple providers to allow the client to make an informed choice. Whenever an analyst has a relationship with another provider, the analyst must disclose this information to clients and related stakeholders. If any referrals involve any fees or incentives, we must document and communicate this to the clients as well (BACB, 2020, 3.13). Analysts must heed caution in these situations as this behavior could be the start of a sticky web of ethical situations. If an analyst receives an incentive for making a referral to a specific provider, is the referral based on the needs of the client or on their own needs and desires? In addition, it is possible we may need to transfer a client to another provider, particularly in situations where the original analyst does not have the skill set the client requires (3.13). When a client transfers from one provider to another (e.g., due to skillset, relocation, the client's request, etc.), the treating analyst must provide relevant data and related information to ensure continuity of care and minimal risk to the client, who is the direct recipient of services.

Callout Box 29:

You are working at an ABA clinic with young children. Many of your clients also receive speech services, most from one company, although several high-quality speech practices are available. In the past, after making referrals to one agency, you received gift cards and bottles of wine for the referrals you made. Imagine you have a new client starting at your ABA organization and during assessment you determine that the client should also receive a screening for speech and language services. When providing the recommendation to the family, you provide only the name of that one company to the family. Which code elements apply to these ethical transgressions? What might you do instead?

Situations will arise that can impact a client's services. These situations can be short or long term, planned or unplanned. One such example is a team member becoming ill and calling out of work. This disruption means we may need to cancel the client's scheduled session, leading to an interruption of the client's routine, and it may serve as a possible barrier to ongoing progress. Turnover is also a very real variable that naturally has a negative impact on a client's ability to make ongoing, robust, and meaningful progress on behavior reduction and skill acquisition targets.

Callout Box 30:

Imagine a situation where a client is receiving 20 hours per week of direct therapy. Their technician quits suddenly and without notice. In this scenario, a large gap in the client's treatment sessions may result, or the client may find themselves in a situation where they are no longer receiving any services at all. As analysts, we must ensure that we have a general plan in place for these various types of situations to help minimize and mitigate the impact that a significant disruption, interruption, or delay can have on a client's outcomes (BACB, 2020 3.14). How could an analyst plan to minimize disruptions for a client receiving 20 hours per week? One idea may be to have multiple technicians working with the client. This way, if one technician leaves, the client will still be receiving a portion of their hours from other technicians on their team.

Of course, an analyst must attempt to avoid an interruption in services (BACB, 2020, 3.14). If a technician becomes ill and calls out for one day, how could the analyst avoid the interruption in services? In such situations, the answer may be as simple as having the analyst rearrange their schedule to provide the services directly. It is also common for funding sources (e.g., health plans) to take an extended amount of time to approve service authorization requests. To address this proactively, agencies may require analysts to submit their assessments a few weeks before the end of the current authorization, to minimize the likelihood that the client will experience a delay or gap in services delivered. Planning ahead for known employee absences and vacations is another step we can take to help ensure continuity in care. In 2020, the field—the world—was confronted with the COVID-19 pandemic, which caused a disruption unlike anything current generations had ever experienced. The pandemic changed the way we provide ABA services. An article titled "A Proposed Process for Risk Mitigation During the COVID-19 Pandemic" by Cox, Plavnick, and Brodhead (2020) recommends strategies for determining how to best continue services for the benefit of clients, but in a way that keeps ABA providers accountable for providing effective treatment during unprecedented times. The authors of this article offer a decision-making process as a way for providers to evaluate risk and reduce harm to clients, while ensuring that they are providing effective treatment. We must weigh the balance of safety of the client, family, and provider against the potential harm that may result from interruptions in services.

An interruption in services will at times be unavoidable and out of the control of the individual analyst. When such a disruption occurs, it will be imperative for analysts and agencies to communicate as quickly as possible with the relevant parties and to work collaboratively to identify and remove barriers so that care can resume as quickly as possible. Analysts must keep clients, families, and stakeholders aware of the situation, inform them of what is being done to resume services, and share any timelines for when services may resume. In some cases a situation may warrant an analyst to make a referral to another provider, such as if they cannot manage the disruptions or if the timeline for resuming services with the current agency becomes too long. Again, as discussed in previous sections of this text, behavior analysts must document all steps taken to resume services (BACB, 2020, 3.14) and the conversations that occur between the provider and the client.

Callout Box 31:

One of your clients receives 30 hours per week of services at the clinic. Data show that the client exhibits increased challenging behavior when unexpected disruptions occur (e.g., a technician cancels the session by calling out at the last minute). Early one morning, one of the technicians who works with the client for 3 hours during a midday session calls into the office and states they are sick and cannot make it to the session. What might the analyst do to avoid this disruption to the client's services?

The BACB outlines six reasons why we may need to discontinue services. *First*, a client may meet all goals and no longer need behavior analytic services. This outcome is the best-case scenario: providing the appropriate density of services and using behavior analytic principles to change behavior so that a client no longer needs our services. The *second* is if a client is not benefiting from service, which may be due to a variety of reasons, such as medical barriers. We must not provide services that are not necessary or directly benefiting the client. The *third* is if analysts, supervisees, or trainees are in a potentially harmful situation or work environment which they cannot resolve within reason. These reasons may include client maladaptive behaviors or an unsafe situation in the home (e.g., unhygienic conditions in the home, harassment from caregivers, violence/weapons). The *fourth* reason is when the client or stakeholder requests to discontinue services. Clients and related stakeholders have the right to discontinue services at any time. Analysts must advocate for the client and provide their recommendation, but ultimately they must follow and honor the client and/or caregiver's decision. The *fifth* reason includes situations in which stakeholders are not following behavior analytic strategies taught to them, which we intend to help them generalize and maintain a client's skills or desired behavior change. Analysts must try to resolve any barriers a stakeholder may have in following the behavior analytic strategies, such as making sure the strategies are reasonable for the stakeholders to implement and ensuring that they are socially valid for that stakeholder. It is important to take a kind and compassionate approach when reconciling differences and when attempting to remove barriers. *Sixth*, without a new agreement in place there may be a discontinuation of services when no longer approved by the funding source.

When clients discharge from services, a responsible analyst will have written discharge plans, which we provide to the client and/or stakeholders at the initiation of the discharge process. Whenever possible, discharge planning should occur prior to the initiation of any discharge process and should include all relevant stakeholders. Once a client begins active steps toward discharge, analysts must document these steps until discharge is complete. Analysts must be aware of funder or organizational requirements, which may also have additional criteria when discharging a client from care, such as time-based requirements or a minimum amount of notice given to the client (e.g., 45 days), if the analyst is the one initiating the discharge.

Callout Box 32:

A new client is starting services. During the assessment process, the analyst reviews how the home environment must be set up for services to take place in the home, including having a clean, separate area for sessions. When the analyst conducts the assessment in the home, nothing seems awry. About two weeks later, the analyst and technician arrive at the client's home for the first day of services. Upon entering the home, they notice that there is trash strewn across the floor and a strong, overpowering odor of stale cigarette smoke. What steps must the analyst take to address this concern? What would you do if the situation does not improve in a reasonable amount of time?

When a service provider discharges a client, the client may not always be exiting care but, rather, transitioning to another provider. A common example of this is when families move or relocate to a new location, such as is often the case with military families. When discontinuation of service occurs, it is essential that we develop a transition plan, which ensures continuity of care for the client, whether switching analysts in the same organization or to an analyst in another organization (BACB, 2020, 3.16). To ensure an ethical transition when designing discharge plans, it is important for analysts to identify the timeline, as well as who is responsible for each step of the transfer. It is our responsibility as analysts to minimize service disruptions, which are likely to occur during transitions. With the client's permission, the analyst will want to connect with the incoming service providers to whom the individual is transitioning. Even if a client is transitioning from one analyst to another in the same organization, even in the same location, transition planning must occur to ensure that we are prioritizing the client's needs, while minimizing the direct, negative impact disruption of services can have on the client's success.

The BACB (2021) has published a document entitled "Continuity of Services: Managing Service Interruptions, Transitions, and Discontinuations." It is a toolkit for analysts to use when documenting service plans for interruptions, transitions, and discontinuations (BACB, 2020, 3.14, 3.15, and 3.16), and it provides information that will help an organization when transitioning and discharging clients. This toolkit includes sample checklists, which an analyst can use as is or modify to meet an analyst's or organization's specific client needs. In addition, it contains three checklists for organizations to use when determining if the procedures in place are adequate for managing client transitions and discontinuation of care: (1) when discontinuing services, (2) when transferring services from one analyst to another in a different organization, and (3) when transferring services between analysts in the same organization (BACB, 2021). It is not a requirement for us to use these checklists, although the BACB does require us to obtain some form of documentation when we transition and discharge clients. The BACB's examples are free, customizable, and easy to use; however, any other documentation you or your organization may design is also acceptable.

In short, Section 3 of our Ethics Code helps analysts to think through responsibilities related to clients and other stakeholders, including initiating, documenting, and discontinuing services. As analysts, at some point in our careers we will have to initiate a relationship with a client and their relevant stakeholders. By focusing on the client's well-being, we can navigate the sometimes tricky situations posed by having multiple stakeholders involved in one case. We can learn to ethically consult with, and make referrals to, other providers. We can also ethically and appropriately discontinue services, whether they are ending or transitioning from one analyst to another.

References

Behavior Analyst Certification Board (BACB). (2020). *Ethics code for behavior analysts.* https://bacb.com/wp-content/ethics-code-for-behavior-analysts.

Behavior Analyst Certification Board (BACB). (2021). *Continuity of services: Managing service interruptions, transitions, and discontinuations.* https://www.bacb.com/wp-content/uploads/2022/01/Continuity-of-Services-Toolkit-220613.pdf.

Cox, D. J., Plavnick, J. B., & Brodhead, M. T. (2020). A proposed process for risk mitigation during the COVID-19 pandemic. *Behavior Analysis in Practice, 13*(2), 299–305. https://doi.org/10.1007/s40617-020-00430-1

Freeman, T., LeBlanc, L., & Martinez-Diaz, J. (2020). Ethical and professional responsibilities of applied behavior analysts. In J. Cooper, T. Heron, & W. Heward (Eds.), *Applied behavior analysis* (3rd ed., pp. 757–782). essay, Pearson Education.

Kelly, A. N. (2018). *Jennifer Lonardo on advocating for appropriate treatment recommendations (Audio podcast episode).* Behaviorbabe. https://anchor.fm/behaviorbabe/episodes/Jennifer-Lonardo-on-Advocating-For-Appropriate-Treatment-Recommendations-e2qj8p.

Kelly, A. N. (2019). *Kate Disney on accessing ABA for military families (Audio podcast episode).* Behaviorbabe. https://anchor.fm/behaviorbabe/episodes/Kate-Disney-on-Accessing-ABA-for-Military-Families-e3h7u8.

Discussion questions

1. Behavior analysts are expected to juggle multiple tasks and responsibilities. List five common expectations of behavior analysts.
2. What is *assent*? How does it differ from *consent*? Why is it important to obtain both assent and consent? When should we obtain assent and consent?
3. What steps can behavior analysts take to ensure that client preferences are embedded into instruction? What might be the harm if a preferred item was paired with a nonpreferred or aversive activity? What steps can behavior analysts take to prevent this detrimental outcome?
4. How can behavior analysts set the stage for ensuring ongoing consultation with medical professionals? What is the benefit to doing so?
5. How can behavior analysts develop or expand their scope of competence (e.g., as it relates to working with older populations, conducting assessments)?
6. When a client is turning 18 years old, what legal and ethical considerations must be made by the behavior analyst?
7. What questions must behavior analysts ask themselves when conducting an initial case review? What are some reasons a behavior analyst or ABA organization might refer a client to another analyst or agency?
8. What components are commonly found on service agreements?
9. What are some common stressors experienced by the families we serve?
10. When there is disagreement between what the behavior analyst prescribes and the health plan authorizes, what steps should the analyst take to advocate on behalf of the client?

Section 4

Responsibility to supervisees and trainees

"Be the most ethical, the most responsible, the most authentic you can be with every breath you take, because you are cutting a path into tomorrow that others will follow."

Ken Wilber

Discussion questions
1. Who determines supervision requirements for behavior analysts and their trainees? (Hint: It is more than one source.)
2. How can behavior analysts improve their supervisory and management skills?
3. Why is there no specific guidance on the number of supervisees a behavior analyst is permitted or recommended to have?

Back to Basics. https://doi.org/10.1016/B978-0-323-85566-2.00005-5

Section 4 of our Ethics Code covers providing ethical supervision. As behavior analysts, we provide supervision not only to our direct care technicians but also often to individuals who are pursuing certification. Both of these situations require us to be familiar with the standards related to supervisions and documentation. Being familiar with the Ethics Code related to supervision can help us navigate the sometimes tricky web of ethical dilemmas.

Behavior analysts must follow supervisory requirements, which may come from the BACB, licensure requirements, funder agreements, and organizational policies. Ultimately, the behavior analyst is responsible for knowing these requirements and following them (BACB, 2020, 4.01). In addition to our clients, we have an obligation and responsibility to our supervisees and trainees. A supervisee includes anyone an analyst is supervising who performs behavior analytic work, such as Registered Behavior Technicians (RBTs), behavior therapists, and other direct support workers. Trainees are those accruing fieldwork experience and working on the requirements for certification. As noted by the BACB (2022), supervisors must oversee at least 5% of the time that an RBT spends providing behavior analytic services. But does this mean supervising for 5% is sufficient for the RBT and the client? Keep in mind that this is only the minimum. Many times, supervisees, trainees, and clients require more supervision than the minimum required. Elisa Cruz-Torres (Kelly, 2019a) presents a podcast episode on the topic of RBTs and ethical considerations. In this Behaviorbabe episode, Cruz-Torres discusses the process of obtaining certification as an RBT, including constraints that technicians face when attempting to obtain competencies in ABA. In addition, she provides advice for technicians and practicing clinicians, including responsibilities and restrictions associated with being a supervisor. Cruz-Torres also offers suggestions for how technicians and their supervisors can overcome barriers that often exist within this dynamic. It is essential for us to investigate and explore these challenges facing practitioners and that we actively, and collectively, seek to resolve them.

It is important to note that the BACB has published an Ethics Code 2.0 specifically for RBTs (BACB, 2022). As supervisors, we must be familiar with that code, as well as our own. The RBT Ethics Code 2.0 references the four core principles as the foundation of both ethics codes and requires RBTs to be familiar with them. As supervisors, it is often up to us to ensure that our supervisees read and understand their code. While many of the RBT ethics standards align with the Ethics Code for Behavior Analysts, there are some differences for supervisors to be aware of and ensure that they understand. The first section, on general responsibilities, reminds RBTs that they must only practice under the supervision of a behavior analyst, remain professional in their work, and work with their supervisor to assess and continue to grow their competence. The second section discusses the RBT's responsibilities in providing direct services to clients. Here, the Ethics Code requires RBTs to be familiar and comply with mandated reporting requirements, follow the direction of their supervisor, complete documentation in a timely manner, and direct all questions to their supervisor. The final section of the RBT Ethics Code addresses the responsibilities to the BACB and their supervisor. This section addresses complying with supervisor and BACB requirements regarding supervision and documentation, maintaining awareness of and following procedures to self-report to the BACB board when necessary, and regularly checking BACB accounts to ensure accuracy. In addition, there is a prohibition against using any intellectual property of the BACB or the organization that employs the RBT. Thus, RBTs cannot share information from their exam or take any proprietary information from their place of employment to use at another location.

In addition to providing supervision to RBTs, behavior analysts also have the responsibility of overseeing and providing supervision to individuals who are obtaining fieldwork hours in pursuit of certification, as well as to individuals certified at the assistant analyst level (e.g., Board Certified Assistant Behavior Analysts [BCaBAs]). In a podcast episode focusing on supervision (Kelly, 2019d), Tyra Sellers discusses supervision within the field of behavior analysis. Sellers addresses topics such as what we mean by *supervision* and who *needs* a supervisor. In addition, she describes what a supervisor needs to know how to do, which she emphasizes includes approaching the relationship with compassion and competence. In this episode, Sellers also shares her personal passion for nature and discusses the benefits for all of us when we stop to smell the roses, or, for that matter, any flower. In a related episode (Kelly, 2019c), Ellie Kazemi also engages in an in-depth exploration of the topic of supervision. Kazemi discusses how to empower students, those we hope will be future analysts, by connecting with them while helping them to highlight their strengths and become aware of their weaknesses. Of particular importance in this episode is Kazemi's further discussion on feedback and conflict resolution in supervision. As supervisors, we must be aware of professional ways to provide feedback to all of our supervisees. In addition, conflict can arise in any relationship and requires behavior analysts to understand both the reason for the conflict and how to appropriately respond and guide the conversation toward productivity.

Students must make numerous decisions when seeking a program in behavior analysis: What will the program cost? What topics are of interest? Which programs are reputable? Is it better to choose on-campus or online coursework? Luckily, there is support for students on how to navigate these questions. One available resource is the "BCBA Examination Pass Rates for Verified Course Sequences," which is published annually by the BACB (2021). This document provides data on the number of first-time examination candidates, as well as overall pass rates for the course sequences. Prospective students can use this document as a guide for decision making. The table of contents includes BCBA Examination Pass Rates sorted by (1) percentage of candidates who passed, (2) percentage of candidates (campus only) who passed, (3) percentage of candidates (online only) who passed, (4) candidate volume, and (5) programs listed alphabetically.

Determining whether to select an on-campus or online program can be a difficult decision, one that not everyone has the privilege to choose because selecting an on-campus option may require relocation. For students who are interested in exploring online instruction, Becky Markovits (Kelly, 2019b) presents how to make the most of an online program. In the podcast episode, Markovits identifies potential barriers (e.g., decreased contact with professors, decreased interactions with classmates and colleagues) and benefits (e.g., time saved on commuting from home, flexible schedule), as well as some suggestions for ways to enhance the overall online learning experience. In a publication evaluating preparation programs, Shepley and colleagues (2017) review differences in behavior analytic programs down to examination pass rates, including an exploration of differences between on-campus and distance learning programs. We encourage prospective students to reference these sources when facing these decisions. However, many individuals seeking to navigate this process may not have readily available access to these resources. Therefore, we encourage each supervisor—both present and future—to familiarize themselves with the perspectives and opinions outlined so that they may offer this guidance to others.

> **Callout Box 33:**
>
> During the COVID-19 pandemic, many funders updated their policies surrounding supervision to allow for more telehealth delivery. While this helped increase the services that were provided during the pandemic, behavior analysts must always examine the decision to provide telehealth supervision from an ethical standpoint. Is this medically recommended for the client? Does it meet the funder's requirements? Does it meet the analyst's organizational requirements? What if it was a brand-new employee starting with a client? A behavior analyst must examine each individual situation and make the best choice.

Behavior analysts supervise others on skills and concepts that are within their scope of competence. This not only applies to the analyst's knowledge of applied behavior analytic principles but also their competence in supervision itself (BACB, 2020, 4.02). Supervision and management of others is a critical skill within this field, yet it is often overlooked in training programs. Competence with supervising requires skill, knowledge, and experience. As analysts, we must continually seek ways to improve our supervisory and management skills, which could come from continuing education events, through mentorship with more senior analysts, and from obtaining diverse experiences across one's career. We encourage early career analysts to seek guidance from seasoned analysts as they begin their supervision journey.

Think about what qualities you appreciated in supervisors you have had when working as an RBT or during your coursework, and seek out mentors who embody those qualities.

Just as behavior analysts maintain a client caseload within their capacity, this too applies to the analyst's supervisory caseload (BACB, 2020, 4.03). There is no clear answer as to what an appropriate supervisory caseload is, and no specific number has been provided by the BACB. That is because everyone's skill set, job responsibilities, life circumstances, and competing contingencies will fluctuate from one point in time to another, as well as from one analyst to another. When assessing one's supervisory caseload capacity, several ethical considerations must be made.

Behavior analysts often supervise trainees or those pursuing fieldwork hours. For many analysts, this is an additional role they take on at their workplace, which is not a role to take on lightly. Think back to your own supervisory experiences as a technician, student, or early career analyst. What characteristics of your supervisors produced the most robust and meaningful supervisory experiences? Remember: You are not simply teaching someone how to do a job—you are being given the responsibility to train, support, elevate, and guide future analysts who are influencing the lives of some of the most vulnerable members of our society. A newer protection afforded by the BACB (2017) requires supervisors to have obtained their credential for one year prior to supervising others, or they must be supervised monthly by an analyst who has at least 5 years postcertification.

Callout Box 34:

A client with 20 hours per week has two technicians who each work 10 hours per week. Can an analyst supervise both technicians during the week? Most likely. What about a client with 20 hours per week who has 10 technicians each working 2 hours with the client? Can an analyst provide sufficient supervision of those technicians during the week? Most likely not. This would probably be a challenging endeavor even for a seasoned analyst, unless this was their only client.

A key part of providing fieldwork supervision is for behavior analysts to train others in areas in which they themselves possess competence. There are times when trainees can establish supervision in their current place of employment. At other times they must find analysts outside of their organization. In addition to BACB ethical considerations, there may be laws and regulations the analyst should be aware of that could influence whether they are the best fit for the individual seeking supervision (BACB, 2020, 4.01). In more than half of the states in the United States, a license is required to provide supervision to a student or trainee. Imagine what could happen if an unlicensed analyst provides supervision to someone in a state where BCBA licensure is required. In addition to potential ethical violations, there could also be legal implications. Imagine what will happen to the analyst if they engage in the practice of behavior analysis in a state where they are not licensed to do so. Consider the hardships this may also create for the trainee, particularly if they are unable to count the hours obtained toward their certification requirements. For reference, we encourage you to seek out information on licensure, which is available on both the BACB and Association of Professional Behavior Analysts (APBA) websites. While reading the laws may seem difficult at first, take time to understand key terms such as *the practice of behavior analysis* and, if needed, seek guidance from others with expertise.

Callout Box 35:

Imagine that you are an analyst who has spent your career working in school settings. You are approached by a trainee who is working in a clinic and seeking a supervision contract with you. Although the trainee does have a supervisor for their direct services work in the clinic, that supervisor is unable to provide fieldwork supervision and no one else in the trainee's organization is available to provide mentoring in accordance with BACB standards. How would you handle this situation as the analyst? What considerations would you make? What protections would you want to put into place if you decided to take on the supervisee?

If, at any time, an analyst finds themself in a position where they cannot effectively supervise additional trainees—whether RBTs or supervisees seeking certification—the analyst must communicate this to their employer (BACB, 2020, 4.03). It is difficult and challenging to uphold the standards of our field while balancing the expectations placed on us by our employers. When placed in these situations, as analysts we must advocate for ourselves, our trainees, and our clients to ensure that we are benefiting others. Unfortunately, there may be situations for which you must decide what is more important: your position at your current place of employment or the career you have chosen, as well as the commitment you have made to your clients.

Providing supervision entails more than mere coaching and teaching. As behavior analysts, we are also responsible for the practices of those we supervise (BACB, 2020, 4.04). Depending on the funding source, services may be billed under the analyst's name, which is one of the reasons it is critical for us as analysts to know what our supervisees and clients are doing. Therefore, adequate, robust, and well-documented supervisory practices are also critical. On one hand, as analysts we can join in the celebration when the clients we supervise achieve success. On the other hand, we must also take ownership and shared responsibility when things do not go according to plan. In addition, analysts are responsible for the public statements made by their trainees as a part of the behavior analytic relationship. This means, among other things, ensuring that technicians are making accurate statements to caregivers.

> **Callout Box 36:**
> Imagine you have a 12-year-old client who receives services in the home. A few times a week, the client engages in aggressive behaviors, which include hitting and pushing others. The former technician who had been working with the client for 6 months recently resigned, and now a new technician is assigned to the case. Consider that the technician is new to the field, has successfully passed the competency assessment, and recently passed the test to become an RBT. Your schedule is packed full, with little flexibility for additional supervision, and you were not anticipating a new team member joining this client's team. You instruct the RBT to review the programs and behavior plan ahead of time, and you inform the RBT that you will check in after the session. Later that afternoon, the RBT calls the office to say they did not know what to do when the client tried walking away from the session, so they grabbed the client, which resulted in the client punching them in the face. What should the analyst do now? If we could turn back time, what might the analyst have done when a new team member was assigned to this case? What ethical codes may have been violated?

It is critical for behavior analysts to provide the amount of supervision needed, based on the skillsets of the supervisee *and* the needs of the client. When analysts are supervising trainees, it is up to the analyst to determine if the trainee can perform certain activities (BACB, 2020, 4.09). The analyst must remember that they are responsible for the work their trainee completes. Through surveying BCBAs who provide supervision to those pursuing field-work hours, Sellers et al. (2019) examine current practices, as well as barriers within supervision. This article reviews recommendations for the field of behavior analysis and emphasizes areas for improvement. Sellers et al. recommend that analysts accept responsibility for their supervision practices, use evidence-based teaching strategies with trainees, and solicit feedback on their own practices. In an earlier, yet related publication, "Training Issues Unique to ASD," LeBlanc et al. (2011) sought to review training issues specific to providing ABA services to autistic individuals. Although ABA is not specific to one particular population, the vast majority of providers deliver services and support autistic individuals. In this paper, the authors highlight the need for practitioners to be trained specifically in autism spectrum disorder (ASD), asserting it is necessary in order to minimize risk and avoid harm.

> **Callout Box 37:**
> An analyst was recently asked to provide consultation with a client's family about toilet training. This client's funding source allows this service to be billed by an individual who is pursuing certification and accruing fieldwork hours. The analyst, being very busy, tells the trainee to conduct the training. In this scenario, the family will get the training they want without waiting for availability in the

Continued

---

analyst's schedule, and the service provided is billable. Due to the analyst's hectic schedule, the trainee's materials are not reviewed ahead of time. What is the potential for harm to the client? What does it mean to be a good behavior analyst? What is the right thing to do?

Pantermuehl and Lechago (2015) examine feedback provided to team members in vivo versus virtually and how it impacts treatment integrity. In their study, the supervisor first used behavior skills training (BST) to teach the error-correction sequence to three behavior technicians. Then, 2 months later, the supervisor attended the technicians' sessions both in vivo and virtually, as well as covertly via video-recorded sessions. Results of this study indicate that both in vivo and virtual supervision resulted in higher levels of treatment integrity than in the covert condition. Treatment integrity of error correction was also higher during these supervision conditions than it was during the study's covert observations. While analysts must meet requirements set by the BACB and other relevant entities, there can be flexibility in the modality, which can still produce robust results. It is critical for us as analysts to individualize our supervision sessions to the needs of our team members and our clients. In addition, we must assess our own competence in providing remote supervision, taking into account our history with using remote supervision, the technician's familiarity with the client, and the client's needs.

We must always document the supervision we provide, which is another requirement set forth by the BACB, as well as by insurance funders and other entities. Appropriately documenting supervision includes completing the documentation, as well as properly storing and disposing of the documentation appropriately (BACB, 2020, 4.05). Documentation must be complete, accurate, truthful, and kept confidential. Analysts/organizations are expected to maintain copies of this documentation for a period of at least 7 years. The BACB also requires that analysts ensure that the documentation of sessions by trainees is complete and accurate. This requires the analyst to regularly review data and session notes for all their clients and to provide feedback and correction where needed.

A behavior analyst provides support and oversees services, which occur both in clinic and in homes. The analyst has a caseload of 10 clients with autism and a team of six behavior technicians. The employer requires all session notes, including supervision notes, to be completed at the end of each day. The analyst does not complete supervision notes one day. No one notices. A second day goes by. A third day goes by. Two weeks go by. The employer then notices that

---

Callout Box 38:—cont'd

paperwork has not been completed. What are the ethical implications? What potential impact could this have on both the analyst and the technicians? What are the implications for the organization?

No one can control everything another person does, but an analyst in a supervisory role must provide the training and supervision necessary to ensure that clients receive access to effective treatment. When situations arise due to the choices of another person, the analyst can show through documentation that appropriate supervision was provided. Remember: Supervising others is more than providing oversight on the clinical work—it also involves using "soft skills" to build rapport with team members. Soft skills are non-technical skills affecting how a person interacts with others. For analysts with trainees, it is critical to teach the importance of these skills. Managing team members is much more than following a simple task analysis like this one: *Step 1: supervise with clients; Step 2: give reinforcement; Step 3: teach new skills; Step 4: document —you're done!* If only supervising others was this easy.

Callout Box 39:

You are an analyst working in a school and providing supervision to behavior technicians who work directly with students. As part of your supervisory practices, you review and teach evidence-based practices. You have documented the supervision sessions and training topics. You overhear the technician telling a teacher you taught them that social stories are evidence based when you did not. What steps would you take next to correct this inaccuracy?

What does it mean to work with compassion and to supervise others with compassion? The answer, just like navigating difficult, ethical situations, is not something one can find in a textbook. It requires combining skills learned from our own training, experience, and reinforcement and punishment histories. As mentioned, soft skills are an important part of the supervisory relationship. As analysts we need to ensure that we develop active listening and communication skills that we can use with others in diverse situations. Listening, compassion, and seeing matters from another's point of view are all skills that will likely lead to better outcomes for our clients. Analysts interact with a wide range of people during their work, including clients, familial stakeholders, third-party stakeholders (including school, insurance, and other organizations), and the team members we supervise. Our field, like all human service fields, *needs* team members to approach clients, their families, our colleagues, and supervisees with kindness and compassion.

Within supervision activities, behavior analysts must include topics related to diversity (BACB, 2020, 4.07). As reported by the BACB, 72% of all BCBAs who shared demographic information identify as white, 9% as Hispanic/Latinx, approximately 6% as Asian, and just over 3% as Black. For BCaBAs, 50% identify as white, 29% as Hispanic/Latinx, 8.5% as Asian, and 3.7% as Black. For both levels of analysts, approximately 85% identified as female (BACB Certificant Data). It is important to know this information and be aware of its influence on the supervision experiences that individuals in our field are providing and receiving. As noted by Conners and colleagues (2019):

> *Although having a more diverse population of behavior analysts working in the field does not necessarily equate to more culturally competent professionals, it may help us recognize the needs of a more diverse client population. Given the increase in the number of behavior-analytic professionals in the field who will be working with diverse populations of clients, the need for training in multiculturalism and diversity issues becomes increasingly important. (p. 768)*

While it is a requirement to include diversity within supervision practices, there is currently no requirement to include diversity training within graduate/certificate programs for trainees or for current analysts when obtaining continuing education credits. So how does an analyst prepare to supervise and train others while incorporating topics on diversity? We believe the answer is by always seeking to learn more, asking questions, seeking out others with diverse experience and histories, listening to supervisees and trainees, and embarking on new or uncharted adventures. Take steps forward, while being guided by science, and be part of shifting the culture within our field and setting an example for your supervisees and trainees to emulate as they themselves transition from student to teacher.

Callout Box 40:

A company organizes training for all analysts and trainees, which includes topics on gender expression and identity. The presenter speaks about offering one's own pronouns to show acceptance of others and describes the difference in asking or stating someone's pronouns versus the person's *preferred* pronouns, with the perspective that accepting others is accepting that a person's pronouns are their pronouns and there are no such things as "preferred pronouns." Later, you are meeting with a trainee and discussing the training. The trainee knows someone who uses they/them pronouns but shares they are planning to refer to that individual as "she" because the persons "looks like a female." What might you do in this situation?

Our own cultural biases impact the supervision we provide to our supervisees and trainees. As behavior analysts, we must become more culturally aware of ourselves and be willing to engage in open discussion with others about how this may impact the services we provide. We must recognize that each of us brings our own lenses to the table: education, culture, gender, sexual orientation, race and ethnicity, religion, and many more. The intersection of these biases will affect how each person views the situation. "Discussion with mentors and colleagues may help behavior analysts learn about themselves and also change their cross-cultural interactions for the better" (Fong et al., 2016, p. 86). Instead of ignoring diversity and culture topics, analysts can ask supervisees and trainees how topics related to diversity may influence the work they are conducting. This questioning challenges supervisees and trainees to think critically and address potential conflict head-on by establishing an awareness and a culture of conversation. Supervising and training others in topics related to diversity requires all parties to evolve. Analysts as supervisors must continue to grow and are responsible for developing those they supervise. Diversity affects supervisees and trainees in their understanding and development in the field of behavior analysis just as much as it affects the clients with whom we work.

Just as analysts must address and cultivate their own skills in the area of diversity, as well as those of their supervisees or trainees, they must help their supervisees develop skills in other areas of the current task list. We recognize that supervisees or trainees learn and acquire skills at different rates, even if multiple supervisees or trainees complete the same training program at the same time. We must be conscious of what tasks our supervisees are currently working on, what they have displayed some growth in, and what they have mastered, as well as what they have not yet attempted. When considering which tasks are appropriate to assign to a supervisee to complete independently, analysts must only assign tasks to supervisees or trainees that are competent in that skill (BACB, 2020, 4.09). For example, a supervisor may have a supervisee assist them with an assessment, perform that same assessment with the supervisor watching and giving feedback, and when the supervisee displays competence, the supervisee may then complete parts of that same assessment without the supervisor directly watching. The supervisor and supervisee must check in throughout the process as the supervisor is ultimately responsible for the assessment. Therefore, analysts must have systems in place to collect data on these skills and assess competency. Performance monitoring must occur for supervisees and trainees, consisting of ongoing data collection of the person's work performance (4.08). Supervision must be documented and include the feedback provided. Throughout supervision, analysts must provide feedback to trainees. We cannot expect trainees to maintain great skills or change skill deficits if feedback is not provided. We must assess the different skills needed to successfully work with the client and the level of skill that the technician or supervisee is displaying for each skill. Feedback may be praise, and it may identify areas for supervisees to improve their skills.

Aubrey Daniels (2009) discusses different ways of providing feedback to others in his book *OOPS! 13 Management Practices that Waste Time and Money (and What to Do Instead)*. One of these is to allow time between positive statements and negative, constructive statements. He highlights avoiding phrases such as "You did a good job but. . . ." As analysts, we are well versed in the principles of reinforcement and punishment. We understand how to increase a behavior that we want to see more often.

Behavior analysts must apply the principles of the field when conducting performance feedback. Providing more frequent praise, both informally, such as when providing praise on the spot, as well as more formally, such as in documented supervision notes and evaluations, is one possible way to increase the behaviors of supervisees.

Daniels (2009) also highlights the sandwich method of feedback and discusses criticism of this method. It can be easy to fall into the sandwich-method trap: positive statement—negative statement—positive statement. We may think to ourselves, "It will soften the blow, right? It will make the other person not feel so bad, right? I do not want to hurt anyone's feelings." Daniels explains that the principles of behavior analysis do not support the sandwich method in changing behavior. We must provide reinforcement and praise for behaviors that we want to continue. Those statements should be separate from feedback for behaviors that need to change. The sandwich method pairs the positive feedback with the negative and may condition all feedback to be aversive. Analysts must instead use the principles of ABA with employees when engaging in performance monitoring and feedback.

Analysts are likely to experience situations with trainees in which a more formal performance improvement plan is warranted. Documentation of previous supervision and feedback can be used to determine if a performance plan may be needed, such as in a situation where the same feedback is provided without any change in the skill by the trainee. Think of it as monitoring a client's progress: If there are no changes to the skill or behavior, changes must occur in the plan. Analysts must develop a goal for the trainee, meet with the trainee to explain the goal, and monitor the trainee's performance on the goal. Performance improvement goals may be SMART goals, which is a style of writing goals following the SMART acronym developed by George Doran (1981): S-Specific, M-Measurable, A-Attainable, R-Relevant, T-Time bound. These are quite like goals we write for our clients.

Callout Box 41:

You are providing supervision in a group home and notice your team member does not have their tablet with them, which is how they record data. You remember that you have provided feedback in the past about this to the team member and also have it documented. This is impacting the client's progress, as there are not enough data to change targets. How would you address this occurrence with the employee? On top of the feedback provided today, your company's policies require a SMART goal since this same feedback has been given three times already. What SMART goal would you develop, and what are the next steps you will take?

Analysts must also evaluate their own supervisory skills, which may come from feedback from supervisees and trainees and through self-evaluation. Analysts must evaluate their clients' outcomes along with supervisee and trainee outcomes. Earlier in this section we discussed having a system in place to document performance feedback for trainees and employees, as well as a way to determine their competencies so we are able to assign tasks within their observed skillset. Analysts can then use those methods to evaluate their own performance: Did the supervisee or trainee meet their goal on time? Are their skills improving, meaning the performance feedback is having its intended effect? Are our trainees and employees gaining any new skills? Ultimately, analysts are responsible for the performance of their trainees and must examine their own supervisory behavior if a change is not occurring. Self-evaluations must be documented, and analysts must use those to make changes within their supervision practices (BACB, 2020, 4.10).

A survey of analysts conducting supervision with trainees was completed by Sellers, Valentino, Landon, and Aiello (2019). The authors identify areas in which supervisors succeed in following expectations related to the supervision of their trainees and what areas are lacking. In the survey, they found the top areas where improvements are needed involve (1) setting clear expectations, (2) conducting ongoing evaluation of the supervisory relationship, (3) using competency-based evaluations and tracking outcomes, (4) directly assessing and teaching professionalism skills, and (5) obtaining feedback on supervisory practices. The analysts in the survey agree that one of the main barriers to providing quality supervision is lack of time. Analysts are responsible for their supervisory volume and must identify when they cannot provide effective supervision (4.03).

During your career as an analyst, situations will arise in which supervision becomes disrupted. We are human and things happen—for example, an analyst gets into a car accident and is hospitalized for a few weeks, an analyst experiences the sudden loss of a parent and must travel to another state, an analyst is pregnant and will be taking leave. For some of these situations that occur suddenly, we are left without time to plan for continuity of supervision (BACB, 2020, 4.11). There are several steps we can take to help with continuity, even in these last-minute occurrences. First, unexpected events highlight the need to keep documentation up to date so that there is less impact on supervision if an emergency occurs. Second, it might be helpful to develop a backup plan that both you and the supervisee discuss to determine what would happen in a short-term situation during which the analyst is no longer available due to an emergency or planned absence. You may also wish to develop longer-term plans with your director, such as always leaving the most recent supervision feedback for RBTs in a specific location and keeping client schedules updated. Any plan for continued supervision must be communicated to all parties.

Callout Box 42:

You are an analyst in a school and are providing fieldwork supervision to a paraprofessional who also works in the school. You have been meeting bi-weekly at school with the trainee. It's now the beginning of May, and school will be out for the summer (3 months) beginning at the end of May. Your position does not require you to work through the summer. What must you do since you are supervising a trainee accruing fieldwork hours? What steps can you take to help your supervisee continue to obtain fieldwork hours if you are not available?

There will also be situations in which the supervisory relationship must be terminated. This, again, must be documented (BACB, 2020, 4.12). If an analyst determines that they cannot continue with their current supervisory volume, they might have to terminate or reduce their supervisory responsibilities. Analysts must minimize the impact on trainees to the fullest extent possible. If an analyst can no longer provide fieldwork supervision to a trainee, this must be communicated with the trainee, and the analyst can work with the trainee to develop a plan so that the trainee can acquire a new supervisor. If an analyst is terminating a supervisory relationship with a supervisee who is also an RBT, this could impact the RBT's ability to maintain active certification. The analyst must document steps taken to minimize potential disruptions to supervisees. Planning for termination of supervision should start as early as possible once the situation becomes known.

Callout Box 43:

You are the only behavior analyst at a company's small, remote location. You have a team of four RBTs who you supervise. You have also been providing fieldwork supervision to one of the RBTs. A new opportunity has presented itself to you, and you have decided to move to a new state in 2 months for a new job. What are your obligations to the RBTs you are supervising? What would you do for the RBT who is accruing fieldwork hours?

Section 4 of our Ethics Code discusses important issues related to the supervision of RBTs as well as those obtaining their fieldwork for future certification. As behavior analysts, we are called upon not only to make treatment recommendations for our clients but to provide effective and competent supervision to our RBTs and supervisees. Many of the skills required to be an effective supervisor are not directly taught in coursework and may require newer BCaBA's to seek out mentorship or continuing education. In addition, we need to be aware of the various requirements for documentation related to supervision. Being familiar with the ethics related to supervision is only a starting place. As analysts, we guide the way for those who come after us, just as our mentors guided us.

References

Behavior Analyst Certification Board (BACB). (2020). *Ethics code for behavior analysts.* https://bacb.com/wp-content/ethics-code-for-behavior-analysts.

Behavior Analyst Certification Board (BACB). (2021). *BCBA examination pass rates for verified course sequences: 2016−2020.* https://www.bacb.com/wp-content/uploads/2021/06/BCBA-Pass-Rates-Combined-211129.pdf.

Behavior Analyst Certification Board (BACB). (2022). *RBT ethics code 2.0.* https://www.bacb.com/wp-content/uploads/2020/05/RBT-Ethics-Code_190227.pdf.

BACB Newsletter. (2017, October). *Newsletters.* Retrieved December 29, 2022, from bacb.com/newsletters.

Conners, B., Johnson, A., Duarte, J., Murriky, R., & Marks, K. (2019). Future directions of training and fieldwork in diversity issues in applied behavior analysis. *Behavior Analysis in Practice, 12*(4), 767−776. https://doi.org/10.1007/s40617-019-00349-2.

Daniels, A. C. (2009). *Oops! 13 management practices that waste time and money (and what to do instead).* Performance Management Publications.

Doran, G. T. (1981). There's a SMART way to write management's goals and objectives. *Journal of Management Review, 70,* 35−36.

Fong, E. H., Catagnus, R. M., Brodhead, M. T., Quigley, S., & Field, S. (2016). Developing the cultural awareness skills of behavior analysts. *Behavior Analysis in Practice, 9*(1), 84−94. https://doi.org/10.1007/s40617-016-0111-6.

Kelly, A. N. (2019a). Elisa Cruz-Torres on RBTs: Ethics and advice (audio podcast episode). *Behaviorbabe.* https://anchor.fm/behaviorbabe/episodes/Dr−Elisa-Cruz-Torres-on-RBTs-Ethics-and-Advice-e35653.

Kelly, A. N. (2019b). Becky Markovits on making the most of online instruction (audio podcast episode). *Behaviorbabe.* https://anchor.fm/behaviorbabe/episodes/Dr−Becky-Markovits-on-Making-the-Most-of-Online-Instruction-e32fca.

Kelly, A. N. (2019c). Ellie Kazemi on the Function of supervision (audio podcast episode). *Behaviorbabe.* https://anchor.fm/behaviorbabe/episodes/Dr−Ellie-Kazemi-on-the-Function-of-Supervision-e4t9be.

Kelly, A. N. (2019d). Tyra Sellers on supervision & stopping to smell the roses (audio podcast episode). *Behaviorbabe.* https://anchor.fm/behaviorbabe/episodes/Dr−Tyra-Sellers-on-Supervision−Stopping-to-Smell-the-Roses-e4m6h4.

LeBlanc, L., Gravina, N., & Carr, J. E. (2011). Training issues unique to autism spectrum disorders. In J. L. Matson (Ed.), *Applied behavior analysis for children with autism spectrum disorders* (pp. 225−235). Springer. https://doi.org/10.1007/978-1-4419-0088-3_13

Pantermuehl, R. M., & Lechago, S. A. (2015). A comparison of feedback provided in vivo versus an online platform on the treatment integrity of staff working with children with autism. *Behavior Analysis in Practice, 8*(2), 219−222. https://doi.org/10.1007/s40617-015-0059-y.

Sellers, T. P., Valentino, A. L., Landon, T. J., & Aiello, S. (2019). Board certified behavior analysts' supervisory practices of trainees: Survey results and recommendations. *Behavior Analysis in Practice, 12*(3), 536−546. https://doi.org/10.1007/s40617-019-00367-0.

Shepley, C., Allday, A. R., & Shepley, S. B. (2017). Towards a meaningful analysis of behavior analyst preparation programs. *Behavior Analysis in Practice, 11*(1), 39−45. https://doi.org/10.1007/s40617-017-0193-9.

Discussion questions

1. Who determines supervision requirements for behavior analysts and their trainees? (Hint: it is more than one source.)
2. How can behavior analysts improve their supervisory and management skills?
3. Why is there no specific guidance on the number of trainees a behavior analyst is permitted or recommended to have?
4. What characteristics of your supervisors produced the most robust and meaningful supervisory experience thus far?
5. What might happen to an individual if they engage in the practice of behavior analysis in a US state where they are not licensed to do so?
6. What factors dictate the amount of supervision a trainee receives?
7. What might the implications be if a trainee is assigned a task outside of their competence? Who is responsible for the work conducted by the trainee? Is it a shared responsibility?
8. Regarding incorporating topics on diversity, how would an analyst prepare themselves to supervise and train others?
9. What is the sandwich approach, and what does Aubrey Daniels say about this as an approach to providing feedback?
10. What are some barriers behavior analysts face when attempting to provide quality supervision?

Section 5

Responsibility in public statements

"If you think about that, you'll do things differently."

Warren Buffett

Discussion questions

1. What is the potential for harm if behavior analysts share information that is embellished or exaggerated for effect?
2. What steps should behavior analysts take when advertising treatments that are not behavior analytic in nature? (Hint: Think of someone who is dual certified.)
3. Why are behavior analysts prohibited from soliciting testimonials from current clients?

Back to Basics. https://doi.org/10.1016/B978-0-323-85566-2.00006-7

91

This section of our Ethics Code applies to public statements, which could include talking with others about the field, giving presentations, putting information on company websites, and even sharing information on social media. Every day, we are faced with opportunities to make decisions on our public statements: Do we correct the person who made a false claim about the field? Do we write a response on social media when we see another behavior analyst break the ethics code by asking for specific advice? Or did we share too much, potentially identifying a client? This section guides you through public statements and those ethical dilemmas with the goal of leaving you empowered to disseminate information about the field.

As behavior analysts, we operate in the best interest of our clients, which means taking the necessary steps to protect the rights of our clients (BACB, 2020, 5.01). We must ensure that we protect client confidentiality in our public statements, which also extends to relationships with stakeholders, supervisees, and trainees (5.02). Inadvertently sharing information could be as easy as being overheard on a phone call with a client's caregiver while in line to pick up coffee or forwarding an email, without checking the entire contents of the email first.

Callout Box 44:

You are at the state capital testifying in support of the need for licensure in your state. Legislators have asked for tangible examples of harm being done by unlicensed professionals. You speak with your clients, who provide you copies of emails, announcements, and meeting notes that address the questions posed by the legislators. However, when you submit this information to the chair and vice chair, you realize you did not redact the documents, which are now public record. What violation has occurred? What can you do to right this wrong? What can you do in the future to avoid revealing confidential information about active clients in your public statements? (BACB, 2020, 5.01, 5.02)

Behavior analysts are ultimately responsible for protecting the personal information of our clients, supervisees, and trainees. When a client ends services, according to both legal and ethical expectations, certain protections must remain in place. Behavior analysts cannot freely share personal and confidential information about current or former clients, just as a physician's office cannot share your information, even if you are no longer actively under their care.

Callout Box 45:

You are being interviewed on the news for your experience and expertise on treating individuals with ADHD. While being interviewed, you are asked to share a success story. You do, being careful not to mention names or the location where the individual lives. You also choose to share about a former client who no longer lives in the same region as you. In this situation, with the protections put into place, do you feel there is any potential of harm to the individual whose story you referenced? Would your answer be different if it were a current client? (BACB, 2020, 5.01, 5.02)

There can be many opportunities and situations in which behavior analysts make public statements about the field of behavior analysis. These statements can help inform others about the field or can serve to help public policy efforts (e.g., insurance reform, licensure). In a publication titled "Spreading the News," Kelly and colleagues (2018) describe and examine how information about behavior analysis is disseminated in different parts of the world, and they detail both successes and challenges, as well as the ethics of effective dissemination. This publication highlights the efforts that have been taken to establish behavior analysis as a stand-alone profession throughout the world.

One major contributing factor to the widespread adoption of behavior analysis has been the passage of autism insurance reform in the United States. While the authors consider these efforts an example of successful dissemination, they also recognize the hurdles consumers continue to face when attempting to access care, including difficulty obtaining a diagnosis, lack of access to care during the school day, and a limited provider network. Some examples of challenges to dissemination include a limited scope of competence, reliance on behavior analytic jargon, misconceptions about our practice, and limited access to reliable funding. Within the article, the authors also provide tips for scientists and practitioners to become more effective disseminators, including the consideration of cultural contexts, knowing one's audience, and using appropriate verbal behavior across various audiences. The authors suggest we stay simple yet precise, while being professional and polite. They suggest that we are proactive: being mindful of our behavior, particularly on social media sites. We must establish boundaries and verify the legitimacy of the information we find online and share with others.

Strategies for
@BEHAVIORBABE
Effective Dissemination

Kelly, M. P., Martin, N., Dillenburger, K., Kelly, A. N., & Miller, M. M. (2018). Spreading the news: History, successes, challenges, and the ethics of effective dissemination. Behavior Analysis in Practice, 12(2), 440–451. https://doi.org/10.1007/s40617-018-0238-8

Consider Cultural Contexts

"Having a thorough understanding of the culture will assist the behavior analyst to connect with their audience, providing examples that are meaningful to them, and lowering the probability that the information will be misunderstood, offensive, or negatively interpreted."

Know Your Audience

"Whilst it is important among scientists to be parsimonious and conceptually systematic, when talking to parents, teachers, professional peers, or government officials, the strict adherence to behavior analytic terminology may run counter to successful dissemination."

Keep it simple, but keep it accurate

Be specific, brief, & concise (Harmsworth et al, 2001).
Speak clearly, accurately, & positively about the field (Johnson, 2017).
Use words or terms that the audience knows, while remaining scientifically correct.

Be Professional and Polite

"Behavior analysts should maintain open lines of communication and be willing to discuss and promote the science. In other words, a behavior analyst should "be a dialoguer, not just a speaker" (Johnson, 2017).

This article provides 10 tips for disseminating effectively. This infographic only reviewed the first four.

Behavior analysts take precautions to refrain from "providing specific advice related to a client's needs in public forums" (BACB, 2020, 5.03), including across social media platforms. There are numerous social media platforms in which information about behavior analysis is shared. Perhaps too often, we see posts from behavior analysts seeking help or asking for suggestions and advice. While likely well intended, this may ultimately be dangerous or, at the very least, detrimental to behaviors that should be in all behavior analysts' repertoires, such as engaging directly with the literature base. Providing access to information online may potentially allow others to circumvent accessing the scholarly literature directly themselves (Carr, 2010). In addition, when an analyst posts a request for help, they risk revealing too much information about their client, thereby risking a breach in confidentiality.

We may also see caregivers reaching out for help, perhaps writing that they are desperate for help and at a loss of what to do. Our desire to help kicks in; you think, "It could be so easy to just give a few tips—I know this could help." However, we cannot give specific advice to individuals outside of a defined professional relationship. Providing support to a family online may prove dangerous, as this might delay them in seeking ongoing support from an appropriate professional. With the little information provided in the post, we would not be privy to the client's full background or family variables, which are needed when making appropriate treatment recommendations. Behavior analysts are permitted to "provide services only after defining and documenting their professional role with relevant parties in writing" (BACB, 2020, 1.04). If behavior analysts see specific advice being provided on social media platforms, we must take steps to address this and correct it. This could include commenting on social media posts about our ethical obligation not to provide advice outside of a defined relationship, as well as privately messaging the person who may have inadvertently violated our ethics code.

Behavior analysts also ensure that the statements we choose to make provide truthful, accurate, and nonexaggerated information. We are ethically obligated to share honest and truthful information without embellishing for dramatic effect (BACB, 2020, 5.03). We need to rely on research and behavioral conceptualization when providing information. In addition, we must ensure that what we say, suggest, or choose to omit will not mislead others who may rely on our statements without verifying them. Imagine a situation in which an analyst does not make a false statement outright but suggests something that may be false, while knowing that others may rely on the statement. What are the potential issues with this scenario? Even by suggesting something to be so, we are affirmatively claiming it to be. Others may not be familiar enough with the field to sift through the statements and suggestions to decipher the truth.

As analysts, we are responsible for the public statements we make when promoting activities relating to the work that we do. There is the expectation that behavior analysts take "reasonable efforts to prevent others (e.g., employers, marketers, clients, stakeholders) from making deceptive statements concerning [our] professional activities" (BACB, 2020, 5.04). Imagine that someone introduces you with the title "Doctor," but you do not hold that title. Why is it important to address this mistake? By correcting it, you ensure that you are being represented accurately to the level of training and education that you hold. Leaving the mistake and allowing others to believe that you are a doctor is misleading, even if it is someone else who says it. This could create a situation in which others feel deceived, which could impact the effectiveness of your consultative services. As with everything we do, we must be sure to document our efforts and attempts to rectify the situation and the outcomes of our efforts. In this situation, sending a follow-up email to the parties involved in the original miscommunication might be involved. Not doing so may put us and our clients at risk (5.04) and could have a negative impact on the field of behavior analysis as a whole.

Callout Box 46:

You are reading posts online on social media, and you see a caregiver asking for help about teaching her child to use the bathroom independently. You know of some great strategies, so you comment in the thread on what she can do to help her child. What is the potential risk of harm for the child? The caregiver? What information could you have provided instead of ideas on specific strategies to try?

With respect to our commitment to behave with integrity, behavior analysts must also be aware of intellectual property laws and must obtain "permission to use materials that have been trademarked or copyrighted or can otherwise be claimed as another's intellectual property as defined by law" (BACB, 2020, 5.05). Intellectual property is defined as "legal property that is the creative property of the mind" (The Law Dictionary, n.d.a). Copyright attaches when the work is "created and fixed in a tangible form," regardless of whether or not the creator files an application with the government (U.S. Copyright Office, n.d.). This requirement to obtain permission before using another's work pertains to public presentations, recordings, websites, podcasts, and so forth. Behavior analysts must obtain permission to use another person's intellectual property. Without obtaining permission, an analyst risks engaging in plagiarism, which is the use of another's work as your own. The results of committing plagiarism can be devastating: loss of employment, loss of confidence in you as a professional, damage to your representation, and even legal actions (The Law Dictionary, n.d.b). Behavior analysts must give credit to others when using their work, ideas, or materials. It is appropriate to give credit to the other person by citing them in the materials. This goes for written work, oral presentations, and even images or photos. Using someone else's work without permission is misrepresenting oneself in experience and knowledge. Just as this paragraph cites the BACB Ethics Code, an online law dictionary, and the U.S. Copyright Office, we must be sure to cite any information we obtain from another source.

While we are likely to automatically think of trademarked or copyrighted materials or a presentation that a speaker gives when thinking about materials we would need to get permission to use, this requirement can also apply to treatment plans and teaching instructions. A lack of trademark or copyright on a specific work does not mean we have permission to use it without giving credit. Another issue that comes into play with copying a treatment plan can be linked back to other codes, such as 2.01 Providing Effective Treatment and 2.09 Involving Clients and Stakeholders. Clients have a right to individualized, effective treatment and must be involved in treatment planning. Therefore, each client's treatment plan and teaching instructions for those goals should be personalized; behavior analysts should not be copying or reusing from another client. Copying a plan from another client can also lead to inadvertently forgetting to change a name or pronouns, leading to possible confidentiality violations on top of insurance funders and caregivers questioning if the plan was written for the client/child.

Callout Box 47:

You attend a presentation sponsored by your local state chapter. At the conference, a presenter speaks on a topic that you are interested in learning more about. The presenter offers to share their slides after the conference with all attendees. Eager to disseminate this information to your colleagues, you use the speaker's slides to present at a monthly analyst meeting, which is recorded. While presenting, you mention that you received the slides directly from the presenter. However, you omit from the discussion the fact that you did not tell the speaker you would be presenting the slides and content verbatim. Consider what is problematic with this and identify different actions that could be taken.

Behavior analysts who possess dual certifications or competence in areas outside of behavior analysis must use caution not to advertise nonbehavioral services as behavioral services (BACB, 2020, 5.06). To be clear, our Ethics Code does not prohibit us from engaging in other therapies or practicing other sciences—only from claiming the interventions associated with these areas are behavioral in nature when they are not. Consider someone who is duly licensed as a speech-language pathologist (SLP) and a behavior analyst. In a podcast episode, Rose Griffin details her journey of becoming an SLP and BCBA (Kelly, 2020). Griffin describes her experiences and shares how they view the two fields as complementary. In talking about a collaboration among multiple professionals, Griffin points out that people contribute different experiences and backgrounds and each brings value to the conversation. In working together and sharing with others across disciplines, ultimately it is our clients that benefit.

While there are certainly many areas where speech services and ABA services overlap, some activities best fit under the purview of speech and language development, rather than behavior analysis. When this occurs, the expectation is for behavior analysts to provide a disclaimer distinguishing those services from the behavioral services. The language provided by the BACB is as follows: "These interventions are not behavioral in nature and are not covered by my BACB certification" (2020, 5.06). The requirement is that we list this disclaimer next to each service the analyst offers that is not in the purview of an analyst or specific to the science of behavior analysis.

With regard to public statements in the form of testimonials, the BACB has revised its policies and position and has provided additional detail on this topic in the most recent Ethics Code (2020). Behavior analysts are still prohibited from soliciting testimonials from current clients for use in advertising meant to be seen by new clients due to "the possibility of undue influence and implicit coercion" (BACB, 2020, 5.07); however, testimonials from former clients may be acceptable under certain conditions (5.08). The use of testimonials with current clients would violate our obligation to protect confidentiality and maintain the privacy rights of clients. Another risk to seeking testimonials from current clients is that clients may feel coerced or pressured, worried that if they say no they will not receive the same level of care as others. The BACB includes information about testimonials from current clients, recognizing that current clients may provide unsolicited testimonials on websites and forums that are outside the control of a behavior analyst. Clients and stakeholders have every right to express their thoughts on their experience with ABA services. The Ethics Code highlights that a behavior analyst cannot use any type of testimonial from current clients in their advertising. Analysts must not share any testimonials that current clients write on websites outside of our control. As behavior analysts, if we become aware that our employer is using current clients' statements on advertising material, we must take steps and document the steps taken to remedy the publication of those testimonials from current clients (5.07).

The Ethics Code includes a separate section from current clients to address testimonials for advertising from former clients (BACB, 2020, 5.08). When a client leaves services, it is possible that the client could come back into services and become a "current client" once again. In deciding whether or not to pursue testimonials from former clients, this is one factor we must consider. The BACB requires that behavior analysts must "identify testimonials as being solicited or unsolicited, including an accurate statement about the relationship between the analyst and the author" who issued the endorsement (5.08). When soliciting testimonials from former clients, we must be clear and thorough when describing where and how these testimonials will be used. We must also inform the individual of any risks associated with the information they provide, as well as their right to revoke or rescind their endorsement at any time and for any reason. Just as with testimonials by current clients, if an analyst becomes aware that their employer has broken this section of the Code, they must take steps to rectify it, documenting their attempts and the outcome.

There is an exception to these requirements provided by the BACB. While we may not solicit testimonials from clients for advertising purposes, we can use testimonials from current and former clients alike for nonadvertising purposes (2020, 5.09). Examples of nonadvertising purposes include applying for grants, raising funds for an organization such as at an autism walk, or disseminating information about ABA when you are not attempting to solicit clients to join your specific company. The purpose of the statements may not be to gain clients but, rather, to inform the general public about behavior analysis. As always, analysts need to be familiar with any laws in their state that may impact their ability to use testimonials.

Callout Box 48:

You are employed by an agency that has solicited testimonials from current clients. Although your boss/employer is not a behavior analyst, you feel uncomfortable with how testimonials are being obtained and how they are being used to recruit new clients, particularly when current client schedules are not maximized. What should you do?

While the BACB (2020) includes specific information on testimonials in our Ethics Code, Phu and Byrne find many examples of wrongdoing in their article "Testimonials on the Web" (2018). During a web search of applied behavior analysis service providers, the authors use a sample size of almost 150 providers. In their review of the websites, the authors find 99 websites that specifically mention BCBAs (therefore meeting the requirement for the Ethics Code) and include testimonials. Of those 99, only 8 include a statement about the testimonials being solicited or unsolicited, meaning they do not meet the BACB's requirements in the Ethics Code.

Phu and Byrne (2018) provide multiple recommendations for both behavior analysts and organizations about testimonials. They recognize that behavior analysts may not have solicited or even known about the testimonials that are being used; they recommend that behavior analysts regularly review content produced by their place of employment. If the behavior analyst then finds an Ethics Code violation within their organization's content, they can address it appropriately. They recommend increasing learning opportunities about the Ethics Code and testimonials, such as more professional development learning opportunities. The authors point out how companies and behavior analysts that use testimonials are likely reinforced by the positive reviews, which in turn likely leads to more clients joining the company. It is therefore up to others in the field to ensure that those who follow the Ethics Code for testimonials are receiving reinforcement and praise for their websites and dissemination of information.

In the most recent version of the Ethics Code (2020), the BACB now includes a section specific to how behavior analysts should behave on social media channels and online platforms. The creation of social media is constantly influencing our society, in both positive and negative ways. It appears it is inevitable for social media to have a role in our practice and profession, particularly in light of our obligation and deep desire to disseminate the science of behavior analysis. Before using social media sites, particularly for professional purposes, there is an expectation that as behavior analysts we have education and possess knowledge about the threats to privacy and confidentiality, particularly as it pertains to social media platforms (5.10). We are strictly prohibited from posting information about our clients on personal accounts. However, there is a bit more wiggle room when it comes to sharing client information on our professional accounts. Before sharing client information on a professional or company page, we must ensure that we (1) obtain informed consent, (2) provide a disclaimer confirming consent was obtained, (3) publish information in ways that reduce the potential for dissemination, such as disabling the share option if possible, and (4) take necessary efforts to prevent and ameliorate the misuse of information we share (5.10). To ensure that we are aware of any potential mishaps or concerns, we must also frequently monitor our social media accounts and channels. It is critical for us to remember that obtaining consent must be voluntary, from fully informed individuals who have the legal and cognitive capacity to make these decisions and to provide this permission. Even when clients do not have the authority to provide legal consent for themselves, we must still seek assent. Equally as important is the knowledge that consent is voluntary and may be revoked at any time without fear of punishment or penalty (5.11).

In "Blurred Lines: Ethical Implications of Social Media for Behavior Analysts," O'Leary and colleagues (2015) present their examination of social media and the ethical implications for behavior analysts. While the article references a previous version of our Ethics Code, the comments and considerations remain pertinent today. Social media quickly grew from helping people foster personal connections to the inclusion of business and advertising. Social media platforms are used by colleges and universities, organizations providing ABA services, personal blogs that disseminate ABA information, blogs on personal experiences, study groups—you name it, it likely exists on a social media platform. In their publication, O'Leary et al. examine information from other associations, such as the American Medical Association (AMA), American Counseling Association (ACA), and American Occupational Therapy Association (AOTA), among others, to review their positions on social media and to make recommendations for what may need to be updated in future versions of our Ethics Code. While exploring Ethics Codes for related professions, O'Leary et al. discovered that, at the time, several associations lacked information specific to social media in their Ethics Codes. The absence of social media references in these Ethics Codes is likely due to being published either before or during the early years of social media, and certainly before widespread adoption of these platforms. Others mention social media either directly in their ethics code or in separate reports, including the ACA and AMA, with the majority highlighting client confidentiality. Another similarity across multiple associations is the recommendation to set boundaries between one's professional and personal use of social media. This is similar to the BACB (2020, 5.10), which includes the importance of publishing professional information on a professional social media page and not publishing information about clients on our personal social media channels.

In their article, O'Leary and colleagues (2015) review different scenarios from social media, providing suggestions for behavior analysts and pointing to specific code elements, even where there is no reference specifically to social media. O'Leary and colleagues note the increase in advice and suggestions being sought online, reminding behavior analysts that we must rely on scientific knowledge, not just what is written online. The authors emphasize the need to maintain a well-defined professional relationship, meaning that if no professional relationship is established with the person on social media, the behavior analyst should refrain from providing specific advice. They provide us with six recommendations for behavior analysts with regard to social media: (1) heavily disguising real clients, (2) avoiding making treatment recommendations, (3) referring readers back to the literature, (4) adding a disclaimer on social media platforms, (5) providing resources such as access to experts in the area, websites with relevant information, and topics to search in the literature, and (6) providing companywide training on the use of social media as part of initial as well as ongoing training that employees receive when starting a new position.

Social media has become an integral part of society. It enables access to a vast variety of people who would not otherwise be convenient geographically, spanning several different generations and regions. Social media provides us with a "cost-effective, immediate, and interactive way to engage with others across the world" (O'Leary et al., 2015, p. 45). For example, it allows us access to one another without much effort and lets us leverage this connection to seek mentors and access experts offline. However, it also presents us with significant challenges. Often, those posting on social media may consider themselves experts in one area or another. As analysts, we should always use caution when evaluating the statements made by others, verifying the sources to the greatest extent possible, getting information from more than one source, and looking for the context of an online conversation to ensure that we are not misinterpreting something someone else says.

ETHICS AND SOCIAL MEDIA

O'Leary, P. N., Miller, M. M., Olive, M. L., & Kelly, A. N. (2015). Blurred lines: Ethical implications of social media for behavior analysts. Behavior Analysis in Practice, 10(1), 45–51. https://doi.org/10.1007/s40617-014-0033-0

HEAVILY DISGUISE CLIENTS

Many characteristics of the individual posting are available online (e.g., location, agency, etc). These characteristics may be enough for others to identify clients, especially if someone reading the post knows the client.

AVOID MAKING TREATMENT RECOMMENDATIONS ONLINE

There is simply not enough information available in online to make a specific treatment recommendation. Clients have the right to assessment and competent behavior analyst. We must not provide recommendations to people who are not our clients.

REFER BACK TO THE LITERATURE

When we provide specific recommendations, we may unintentionally encourage others to circumvent the literature. Instead, suggest topics and researchers the individual can look more into. This encourages an evidence-based approach that is specific to the client the analyst is serving.

WRITE A DISCLAIMER

Be clear that you are not providing a specific treatment recommendation or clinical or legal advice. It's best to be proactive!

PROVIDE RESOURCES

Share ideas, links to literature, helpful websites, and experts in the field or specific subject matter area.

SET POLICIES / TRAIN OTHERS

Ongoing training will allow agencies, technicians, and analysts to continually revisit and revise what "appropriate" social media looks like.

Behavior analysts are likely to encounter situations daily where they can share information about behavior analysis. From being asked at an appointment about our occupation, to speaking with a prospective client, to advocating for legislation, and even on social media, there is no shortage of opportunities to disseminate information about the field. Behavior analysts must do so truthfully, without exaggerating or falsifying information, and must always ensure client confidentiality.

References

Behavior Analyst Certification Board (BACB). (2020). *Ethics code for behavior analysts.* https://bacb.com/wp-content/ethics-code-for-behavior-analysts.

Carr, J. E., & Briggs, A. M. (2010). Strategies for making regular contact with the scholarly literature. *Behavior Analysis in Practice, 3*(2), 13—18.

Kelly, A. N. (2020). Rose Griffin on being an SLP & BCBA (audio podcast episode) (Host) *Behaviorbabe* https://anchor.fm/behaviorbabe/episodes/Rose-Griffin-on-Being-an-SLP—BCBA-e4chba.

Kelly, M. P., Martin, N., Dillenburger, K., Kelly, A. N., & Miller, M. M. (2018). Spreading the news: History, successes, challenges and the ethics of effective dissemination. *Behavior Analysis in Practice, 12*(2), 440—451. https://doi.org/10.1007/s40617-018-0238-8.

O'Leary, P. N., Miller, M. M., Olive, M. L., & Kelly, A. N. (2015). Blurred lines: Ethical implications of social media for behavior analysts. *Behavior Analysis in Practice, 10*(1), 45—51. https://doi.org/10.1007/s40617-014-00330.

Phu, W., & Byrne, T. (2018). Testimonials on the web: Evidence for violations of the professional and ethical compliance code for behavior analysts. *Behavior Analysis: Research and Practice, 18*(4), 419—424. https://doi.org/10.1037/bar0000135.

The Law Dictionary. (n.d.a). *Definition of intellectual property.* https://dictionary.thelaw.com/intellectual-property.

The Law Dictionary. (n.d.b). *What are some consequences of plagiarism?* https://thelawdictionary.org/article/what-are-some-consequences-of-plagiarism.

U.S. Copyright Office. (n.d.). *Copyright in general.* https://www.copyright.gov/help/faq/faq-general.html#:~:text=When%20is%20my%20work%20protected,of%20a%20machine%20or%20device.

Discussion questions

1. What is the potential for harm if behavior analysts share information that is embellished or exaggerated for effect?
2. What has led to the widespread adoption of behavior analysis in the United States?
3. What are three hurdles consumers face when attempting to access care?
4. Why is it dangerous to provide advice to individuals online who are not our clients?
5. What steps should behavior analysts take when advertising treatments that are not behavior analytic in nature? (Hint: Think of someone who is dual certified)?

6. Why are behavior analysts prohibited from soliciting testimonials from current clients?
7. Why are behavior analysts prohibited from posting information about their current clients on personal social media accounts?
8. What steps must be taken to ensure protection of clients when sharing images or information about them on a professional or company social media page?
9. What is the importance of referring to the literature when someone asks a treatment question online?
10. What are the benefits to embedding portions of the Ethics Code into company policies and employee handbooks?

Section 6

Responsibility in research

"It takes less time to do a thing right than to explain why you did it wrong."

Henry Wadsworth Longfellow

Discussion questions
1. When conducting research, behavior analysts must take steps to protect clients. Who must provide approval for the specific research to be conducted?
2. When conducting research, it must benefit the client, as well as inform practices in the field. What protections must be made when professional services are being offered as an incentive for research participation?
3. Why is it important for behavior analysts to disclose and address any potential conflicts of interest with all potential research participants and stakeholders?

Section 6 of our Ethics Code (BACB, 2020) focuses on our responsibilities when conducting research. As with other sections of our Code, the focus is on

Back to Basics. https://doi.org/10.1016/B978-0-323-85566-2.00007-9

what is best for the client. In research, we must be aware of the legal standards surrounding research with human subjects, including any applicable state and federal laws. We must also obtain informed consent from the participants or their legal guardians and take care to guard the confidentiality of our subjects. Ensuring that we follow these necessary safeguards will assist us in maintaining our focus on what is in the best interest of the client. Analysts are also required to ensure that data are accurately collected, described, and displayed in ways that will not lead to misinterpretation. We must disclose any possible conflicts of interest and give appropriate credit to everyone who contributes to the study.

To continue to elevate our field and outcomes we achieve for our clients, there is a need for ongoing research. However, there has been some disagreement on whether university programs should teach students to be researchers. In an article by Richard Malott (1992) titled "Should We Train Applied Behavior Analysts to Be Researchers?" the author analyzed the job market for behavior analysts and found that a "large percentage of behavior-analyst alumni of our graduate programs work mainly as practitioners, not as teachers and researchers" (p. 85). The author went on to discuss how preparing graduate students to be researchers does not give them the tools they will need to be practitioners and supervisors, which most will ultimately do. Malott also points out that few graduate programs produce successful researchers, with only 2 percent of doctoral-level analysts publishing with any frequency at the time of the article. Malott then concludes that the few graduate professors who are successfully producing researchers should continue, but the majority of professors should redesign their thesis and dissertation requirements to prepare practitioners rather than publishers.

In a follow-up article, Dennis Reid (1992) agrees that few programs are producing successful researchers, but he comes to a different conclusion than Malott did: Programs need to make changes to be more effective at teaching students to be researchers. Reid's article, "The Need to Train More Behavior Analysts to Be Better Applied Researchers" states several reasons why it is important that students learn to be better researchers, including (1) the ability to recognize and avoid implementing problematic research in their daily practice and (2) performing research as a practitioner can lead to better service provision. Reid echoes Malott's suggestions that the focus on research can include a focus on, and potentially an internship in, applied research. However, Reid emphasizes the need to continue to train analysts to be researchers rather than making a more drastic change suggested by Malott. Clearly, the need for research exists; however, there are different approaches to ensuring competence in research methodologies.

As behavior analysts, we know our clients have a right to effective treatment. But how do we know that a treatment we are considering will be effective? Where do we look to find more information when a caregiver approaches us and asks us to, for example, try equine therapy with their child? Two resources that help assist practitioners in evaluating the effectiveness of different treatments related to autism are the Association for Science in Autism Treatment (ASAT, 2022) and the National Autism Center's National Standards Project. ASAT provides a website that is regularly updated with treatment information, monthly newsletters, interviews, and clinical information. It is a helpful resource when trying to decide if a treatment may be effective for a client. The National Standards Project is a longer-term study that categorizes treatments as effective, needs more research, or is not effective. Its resource guide is published every few years with updated information and is available for free on the website. Of course, at times we may be conducting our own research. The remainder of this section focuses on instances when we are designing and implementing a research study.

When conducting or participating in research, behavior analysts "plan and conduct research in a manner consistent with applicable laws," which means being familiar with and following the requirements related to working with an Institutional Review Board (IRB) for starters (BACB, 2020, 6.01). IRBs are independent review committees that assess the proposed research, including risks to the participants. IRBs often have an association with universities, though there has been an increase in independent boards accredited by the Association for the Accreditation of Human Research Protection Programs (AAHRPP, 2022).

Both federal and state laws protect human subjects in research. The U.S. Department of Health and Human Services (HHS) Office for Human Research Protection has issued policies protecting individuals who are enrolled in research studies. These regulations are referred to as the Common Rule. While this law is only applicable to research performed by the federal government or using federal funds, several states, including Maryland and Florida, have adopted these or similar regulations as state law (Tovino, 2020). Of note is Subpart D of the Common Rule, which lists out the requirements for research using children, including the need to obtain the assent of the child as well as informed consent from the legal guardian. California's Protection of Human Subjects in Medical Experimentation Act includes a bill of rights for participants, requiring "experimentation shall be undertaken with due respect to the preciousness of human life and the right of individuals to determine what is done to their own bodies" (2013, Section 24171). As behavior analysts, we have an obligation to be familiar with and follow laws when we engage in any research. As laws can change frequently, it is important that we check relevant state and federal laws prior to beginning any new study, even if we have been conducting research for many years. Anytime we are conducting research, whether independent or a part of ongoing service delivery, we ensure that approval is sought from a formal research review committee (BACB, 2020, 6.02).

"Behavior analysts conducting research in the context of service delivery must arrange research activities such that client services and client welfare are prioritized" (BACB, 2020, 6.03). Consider this requirement and its relevance when selecting single-subject research designs. When we are conducting research, we want to ensure that we eliminate potential confounds, select the most convincing design, and present the most compelling visual display. However, we must never allow any of those ambitions to supersede our commitment to our clients, and we must ensure that their welfare is held above all else. Perhaps one of the most compelling research designs, which allows us to demonstrate a functional relation, is a reversal or A-B-A-B design. However, once we identify an effective intervention, we must consider whether it is ethical for us to remove the support, simply for the purposes of demonstrating a clear functional relation. Another example might be when researchers utilize a multiple-baseline design, across clients, settings, or behaviors. With a multiple-baseline design, intervention is delayed or withheld until an effect is achieved for the first client or within the first condition. If the behavior of interest is harmful and intervention is necessary, it may not be ethical for us to delay implementation. "In these situations, behavior analysts must comply with all ethics requirements for both service delivery and research within the Code" (BACB, 2020, 6.03).

Callout Box 49:

You are working with a client with limited verbal communication. You decide you want to do some research on which is the best method of communication for this client, as well as several others who are not developing vocal speech. You design a study, go through an IRB, have the appropriate consent, and are ready to begin. In this project, you are comparing sign language and Picture Exchange Communication System (PECS) . However, this client begins to increase their vocalizations and engages in aggression when you try to prompt them to sign. They are now in the PECS phase; however, your study calls for a reversal where you are to reintroduce sign language with the client. You want to continue your study but are concerned with the increase in aggression. What do you do? Use the questions posed by Freeman, LeBlanc, and Martinez-Diaz (2020): "What is the right thing to do? What is worth doing? and What does it mean to be a good behavior analyst?".

In their article "Establishing Consumer Protections for Research in Human Service Agencies," LeBlanc, Nosik, and Petursdottir (2018) review some best practices for ensuring consumer protection in research. They review the definition of *research* (versus *treatment evaluation*), present the requirements of research review committees, and challenge readers (scientists-practitioners) to uphold consumer protections in their research. They recognize the need for a resource to be available to help guide organizations in growing and building their research in the field. LeBlanc and colleagues write, "[W]hether the research generated in applied settings is published or not, the scientist-practitioner is much better equipped to deliver the most effective treatment when experimental control is used to determine effectiveness" (p. 454). Clients must always have the right to access effective treatment, even in research. Therefore, it is important that we regularly evaluate the effectiveness of our treatments and make changes when necessary.

An additional resource that examines ethical research is a new book by Cox, Syed, Broadhead, and Quigley (2022) titled *Research Ethics in Behavior Analysis: From Laboratory to Clinic and Classroom*. This book is a resource guide not only for the experienced behavior analyst researcher but also for the early career behavior analyst needing to expand their knowledge in the field of research.

Regarding conducting research, behavior analysts obtain informed consent and assent (BACB, 2020, 6.04). The informed consent must be obtained from the client or the legal guardian and must conform to the conditions required by the IRB. Informed consent requires that we provide the participants or their legal guardians with information regarding the possible benefits and risks of participating in the study, specify that consent or lack of consent will not impact the client's ability to receive services, and explain the right to revoke consent at any time. In addition, to the extent possible we must obtain the assent of the participants themselves. As with obtaining assent to treatment, this may take many different forms, depending on the client. When we become aware that data previously collected during regular service delivery may be disseminated, we must then obtain the informed consent of the client, stakeholder, and/or trainees affected.

Behavior analysts provide protection of client confidentiality when engaging in research (BACB, 2020, 6.05). We make all attempts to prevent the disclosure of confidential or identifying information. When presenting research, we change client names and disclose only information required to make informed decisions based on the research. This may include aggregated statistics on gender, race or ethnicity, and ages of participants.

Callout Box 50:

You have finished your research study using eight participants. You want to display their data and present your research at your local chapter's ABA conference. You have permission to present from all participants' guardians. You put your poster together using fake names for your clients; however, you include individual age, ethnicity, and gender for each client. Your employer asks that you put the company's name on your poster. You live in a small community and are afraid that some individuals at the conference may be able to figure out who the clients are based on your employer and the identifying information you have used. What are the problems associated with including the employer's name? What other steps could you take to ensure that you prevent the disclosure of confidential information?

Just as we practice within our scope of competence, we need to ensure that we are competent in the areas we are assessing and in the role we play in conducting research (BACB, 2020, 6.06). First, the Ethics Code states that behavior analysts should not conduct any research independently until we conduct research under a supervisor. That means if an analyst is new to research, they must find a mentor who has conducted studies previously to ensure that the analyst gains competency in research studies. Second, if an analyst has conducted research in a particular area and now wishes to do research on something completely new, they must reach out to others competent in the new area as mentors or partners in their research. In addition, the Ethics Code states that the researcher is accountable for the ethical conduct of any other individual involved in the study. Therefore, it is important to adequately train all assistants and monitor their work to ensure that they are also complying with ethical expectations for conducting research.

When conducting research, we are ethically obligated to disclose and address any potential conflicts of interest, which may range from personal to financial to organization or service related. This information is also disclosed during publishing and editorial activities (BACB, 2020, 6.07). A conflict of interest may exist when an analyst receives funding from a particular organization for the study, and there is reason to believe the outcome of the study may be influenced by the funding source. Many times, the conflict does not influence the study but the lack of disclosure may lead others to believe that the study may be biased. The existence of a conflict does not indicate that the study is not valid; however, disclosure shows that additional steps were taken to safeguard the integrity of the study.

When participating in research with others, as is often the case, behavior analysts must ensure that we give appropriate credit to others who contributed to the project or publication. Depending on the contributions, contributors may be credited as authors or may be part of an author's note acknowledging the assistance of other individuals. While a technician who implements part of a procedure and collects data may not be a co-author, it is important to acknowledge them in the publication. Furthermore, "authorship and other publication acknowledgments accurately reflect the relative scientific or professional contributions of the individuals involved, regardless of their professional status (e.g., professor, student)" (BACB, 2020, 6.08). When multiple authors contribute to a study, the order of authorship is generally dictated by the amount of work each individual contributed to the study, with the person making the biggest contribution first and the one with the smallest contribution last.

Callout Box 51:

You have been invited to participate in a publication on public policy and advocacy because your involvement in these activities is widely known and well respected. You agree to participate with two other individuals, one of whom is a student completing their doctorate program. You and this student work together closely on the project, and together you complete the lion's share of the work. The third author, who originally organized the partnership, has only been available to provide some opinions and light editing on the sections you and the student have written. When the project is complete and you are ready to submit the publication for consideration, you learn that you are listed as the third author. What potential violations have occurred? What can you do to address and resolve your concerns? What steps can you take in the future to avoid finding yourself in a similar predicament?

As discussed earlier in Section 5, behavior analysts provide proper credit when citing others' work and "do not present portions or elements of another's work or data as their own" (BACB, 2020, 6.09). To do otherwise would be plagiarism, which could result in costly lawsuits for infringement on another's intellectual property. Behavior analysts only republish their own data or reference their own work when accompanied by proper disclosures. The *Publication Manual of the American Psychological Association*, 7th edition (2020) defines self-plagiarism as "the act of presenting one's own previously published work as original" (p. 21). Therefore, it is important to include a disclosure when republishing to inform the reader that this was previously published. Purdue's Online Writing Lab (n.d.) contains a plethora of resources for identifying and avoiding plagiarism. It is a good website to visit for anyone questioning whether what they are writing falls in the category of plagiarism or how to avoid the potential legal and ethical consequences associated with copying someone else's work.

Just as we are required to follow laws, regulations, and BACB rules regarding keeping and transmitting records, analysts must also be sure to follow these same laws and rules when dealing with data collected during a research study (BACB, 2020, 6.10). In addition, we must follow any guidelines provided by the IRB that approves the study. Analysts must store, transport, and destroy records in accordance with the strictest guidance. So if the law requires retention for 3 years but the IRB states you must maintain the records for 5 years, the analyst must keep those records for 5 years. When permitted, the analyst will make a deidentified copy or summary of the records, such as a graph or report with no identifiers, prior to destroying the physical records.

Finally, analysts performing research must take all steps to ensure that their data are accurate and not misleading (BACB, 2020, 6.11). Analysts must ensure that data are not fabricated and records are not falsified for any aspect of a study. When presenting research, we must "plan and carry out [our] research and describe [our] procedures and findings to minimize the possibility that [our] research and results will be misleading or misinterpreted" (BACB, 2020, 6.11) When we provide a thorough description of our research methods and our study findings we will be "do[ing] a thing right," meaning we are less likely to have to defend our work or rewrite our study in the future (as noted in this section's opening epigraph). If an analyst finds that some part of their published works is incorrect, they must take steps to correct this information with the publisher. Generally, research data should be presented as a whole. At times, however, this is impossible or unfeasible. For example, a participant may withdraw consent so their data may not be included. Whenever research cannot be presented as a whole, the researcher-practitioner must take steps to disclose this and provide a rationale and description for what was excluded.

Section 6 of our Ethics Code is relevant to practitioners conducting research with human subjects. We must take steps to ensure protection of the client's data and ensure that we are familiar with and follow any and all applicable laws. We are familiar with the subject we are researching, the methods we are planning to use, and the process of research generally, or we obtain a mentor or partner in our research. Throughout all things we do, we must ensure that we are benefiting others, approaching situations with curiosity, treating others with dignity and respect, behaving with integrity and honesty, and ensuring our competence by remaining current and knowledgeable. We must be open to changing our opinion when presented with new, compelling information.

References

American Psychological Association (APA). (2020). *Publication Manual of the American Psychological association* (7th ed.) Author.

Association for the Accreditation of Human Research Protection Programs (AHRPP). (2022). *Home page.* https://www.aahrpp.org.

Association for Science in Autism Treatment. (2022, June 29). Home page https://asatonline.org.

Behavior Analyst Certification Board (BACB). (2020). *Ethics code for behavior analysts.* https://bacb.com/wp-content/ethics-code-for-behavior-analysts.

California Code. (2013). *Health and safety code − HSC. Division 20. Miscellaneous Health and safety Provisions. Chapter 1.3. Human experimentation.* Justia Law https://law.justia.com/codes/california/2013/code-hsc/division-20/chapter-1.3.

Cox, D. J., Syed, N., Brodhead, M. T., & Quigley, S. P. (Eds.). (2022). *Research ethics in behavior analysis: From laboratory to clinic and classroom.* Elsevier Academic Press.

Department of Health and Human Services (HHS) Office for Human Research Protection. (2021, December 15). *Subpart D - additional protections for children involved.* https://www.hhs.gov/ohrp/regulations-and-policy/regulations/45-cfr-46/common-rule-subpart-d/index.html.

Freeman,T., LeBlanc, L., & Martinez-Diaz, J. (2020). Ethical and professional responsibilities of applied behavior analysts. In J. Cooper, T. Heron, & W. Heward (Eds.), *Applied behavior analysis* (3rd ed., pp. 757−782). essay, Pearson Education.

LeBlanc, L. A., Nosik, M. R., & Petursdottir, A. (2018). Establishing consumer protections for research in human service agencies. *Behavior Analysis in Practice, 11*(4), 445−455. https://doi.org/10.1007/s40617-018-0206-3.

Malott, R. W. (1992). Should we train applied behavior analysts to be researchers? *Journal of Applied Behavior Analysis, 25*(1), 83−88. https://doi.org/10.1901/jaba.1992.25-83.

National Autism Center at May Institute. (2022). *National standards project.* https://nationalautismcenter.org/national-standards-project.

Purdue Writing Lab. (n.d.). *Plagiarism overview.* https://owl.purdue.edu/owl/avoiding_plagiarism/index.html

Reid, D. H. (1992). The need to train more behavior analysts to be better applied researchers. *Journal of Applied Behavior Analysis, 25*(1), 97−99. https://doi.org/10.1901/jaba.1992.25-97.

Tovino, S. A. (2020). Mobile research applications and state research laws. *Journal of Law Medicine & Ethics, 48*(S1), 82−86. https://doi.org/10.1177/1073110520917032.

Discussion questions

1. When conducting research, behavior analysts must take steps to protect clients. Who must provide approval for the specific research to be conducted?

2. When conducting research, it must benefit the client as well as inform practices in the field. What protections must be made when professional services are being offered as an incentive for research participation?

3. Why is it important for behavior analysts to disclose and address any potential conflicts of interest with all potential research participants and stakeholders?

4. When is it important to provide proper credit to project contributors or co-authors? What might this look like when the analyst is presenting on this scholarly work at a conference?

5. What is the benefit to being willing to change our opinions when we are presented with new information?

6. What steps must be taken when an analyst wishes to disseminate previously collected data?

7. What is self-plagiarism, and why is it important to use appropriate disclosures?

8. What sources must we look at when determining how long we must retain documents related to research?

9. What is an Institutional Review Board (IRB), and why is it important to consult one when performing research on human subjects?

10. When it is not possible to present the study in its entirety, what steps must a behavior analyst take to ensure that the study is not misinterpreted?

Conclusion

"Without "ethical culture" there is no salvation for humanity."

Albert Einstein

Throughout the discussions in this text, we circle back to the concept that you will not find the answers you seek neatly packaged in a textbook, as the situations you will encounter and the scenarios you navigate will vary and fluctuate. No two situations will ever be identical. Often, you will discover there is more than one way to approach a situation, and while that decision is yours to make, the tools we provide equip you with the tools and resources you need to navigate the challenges that lie ahead.

As we have discussed throughout this book, ethical practice is very rarely a black-and-white issue. Ethical dilemmas come with a wide variety of nuances,

Back to Basics. https://doi.org/10.1016/B978-0-323-85566-2.00008-0

requiring us to make individualized judgments based on the factors in that particular situation. We remind you of the three questions from Freeman, LeBlanc, and Martinez-Diaz (Cooper, 2020) as one starting point for assessing what to do when faced with an ethical challenge. "What is the right thing to do? What is worth doing? and What does it mean to be a good behavior analyst?" (p.757). These questions can give you the tools needed to guide your decision on what to do when you are facing an ethical dilemma. In addition, we encourage you to use the six-step decision-making process, which we hope you are comfortable using in a wide variety of situations. As a reminder, these six steps are (1) identifying if there is an ethical concern, (2) brainstorming solutions, (3) evaluating solutions, (4) determining if there is a solution/clear course of action, (5) implementing the solution with fidelity and integrity, and (6) reflecting on our results (Rosenberg & Schwartz, 2019).

We also ask you to reflect back on the core principles from our Ethics Code: benefit others; treat others with compassion, dignity, and respect; behave with integrity; and ensure competence (BACB, 2020). These principles can help you navigate some tricky situations by reminding you of what is most important in all that we do: our clients. When we focus on acting in the best interest of our clients, using compassion when working with others, practicing within our scope of competence, gaining new competence as needed, and behaving ethically, even when no one is watching, we are likely to make decisions that align with our Ethics Code.

In Section 1, we discussed the importance of involving our clients in treatment planning, which is particularly necessary when we think about consent and assent from our clients. We want our clients to work on goals that are going to change their lives, not on goals that are irrelevant. We also discussed the need to remain abreast of the evolving expectations in our field and increasing your competence in different areas by attending conferences, reading emails and newsletters from the BACB, getting involved in your state ABA chapter, referring back to our Ethics Code, and reading research articles. In addition, as an early career analyst, it may be helpful for you to maintain a relationship with your previous mentors or find new ones to help you increase your competence. Of course, we also feel extending one's competence applies to seasoned analysts as well as to early career practitioners. Our field is not an easy one, and the more we immerse ourselves in the communities around us, the more likely we are to be successful as curious and compassionate analysts.

Whenever possible, we suggest that you find ways to embed ethics into company practices and policies. As an early career analyst, you may have little say over these policies and practices, but a good start is to ask questions about how a policy fits in our Ethics Code. Being knowledgeable about our Ethics Code will help you formulate questions and work with your company to be as ethical as possible. Analysts must always take steps to decrease the risk of multiple relationships by setting clear boundaries with families, noting what is a part of the relationship and what is outside of an ethical relationship. We also urge you to spend time learning about conflict resolution to help prepare you for those moments of conflict with the families you work with, the school districts clients attend, the related service providers seeing your clients, or your client's funding source. Conflict is inevitable, as we are all human. It is imperative that we learn to navigate these conflicts before they damage our relationships or our ability to work with a client. Keeping conversations focused on what is best for the client, realizing we are all there to make the best life for that client, and treating others with compassion and empathy are all steps toward resolving conflicts in the best interest of our clients.

In Section 2, we introduced the six rights to effective treatment. In general, our clients have the right to make meaningful progress on goals that are important to them. Thinking back to the concept of social validity, it is important that we work with the client, caregivers, and other stakeholders to ensure that we are creating goals that are socially valid in the client's unique situation—we are not going to teach a child in a tropical climate to put on snow boots. We also must consider the client's preferred reinforcers and ways to expand a limited repertoire of reinforcers, taking particular care not to rely on fatty or sugary foods. When looking at reinforcers, it is important to stay focused on the client's interests and keep those front and center as you look for additional activities that clients may enjoy. Consider both the short-term and long-term effects of your treatment. For example, a client with limited communication and social interactions, who is not yet independent in daily living skills may not need to work on academic-based skills. Imagine you are only given two treatment authorizations or one IEP year to achieve the progress your client needs to make. In this case, we must prioritize treatment goals, keeping the number of goals reasonable, ambitious, and achievable. We must think about what goals are going to give the client the maximum amount of impact in a short time and work on those goals first.

When considering treatment goals, select skills that the client can maintain in the natural environment. The programs that do not require contrived main-tenance trials to maintain are more likely for the client to continue doing long after we are finished working with them. As noted when discussing cultural competence and humility in Section 2, competence is not something that can be achieved and disregarded—it is an ongoing process. Observing our clients across settings and interviewing several relevant stakeholders will allow us to develop the most comprehensive and effective treatment plan possible.

Ensuring that all children with autism or other disabilities have access to in-surance was a hard-fought battle, requiring decades of advocacy. Those of us in the trenches of advocacy would discuss how "Today's problems are yesterday's dreams," recognizing that the things we dreamed of in previous years require us to continue the fight long after (Kelly, 2015). We truly have seen so much progress when it comes to autism insurance mandates; however, as with all things, we need to continue to advocate for the best outcomes for our clients. When practicing, it is important to build a community of other analysts and to have resources and ex-perts you can rely on. However, remember that some things cannot be discussed in a large group (e.g., Sherman Antitrust Act). It is important to be aware of laws related to your practice and to ensure that you are following them.

In Section 3, we focused on some of the challenging aspects of being a behavior analyst. If we do not choose our language carefully and make what we say understandable to those who are not behavior analysts, we may contribute to disagreements or misunderstandings about our field. As analysts we are responsible for the language we use to describe our science, replacing some common misconceptions (e.g., "It is just dog training" or "Reinforcement does not work") with the truth. Being a behavior analyst is a big responsibility. We are changing lives, hopefully for the better, and we need to understand the research and communicate it in a way that consumers and funders can understand. Communicating clearly also includes visually displaying data, effectively, in a way that paints a picture or tells the story.

Our data displays should be understandable to families, funders, and other providers, allowing them to weigh in on other possible factors that are occurring, such as a need to start medication or a giant growth in communication due to all providers working together. We never blame our clients for their lack of progress. We also never blame a broken system. As behavior changers, we are responsible to make the changes needed to our client's programming to ensure progress. We are also responsible for looking at the environment to identify factors we can change or impact.

At all times, we must operate in the best interest of our clients; however, we also must avoid making assumptions as to what is in the best interest of another individual. Some skills we teach are negotiable, such as learning to ride a bike. Others are not, such as following rules related to safety, like not running into the street, and wearing clothing when outside of the home. Regardless, the process and procedures we use should be heavily influenced by client preferences and requests. We must remain aware of possible unintended effects of our treatment and take care to avoid them—for example, imagine withholding someone's favorite song or food until they perform a less desired activity: Will this have the desired effect of encouraging the skill or behavior we are targeting? Will it have the undesired effect of tarnishing the favorite activity or item that has been paired with a potentially aversive demand? What steps have we put in place to monitor for these effects? What protections have we and must we continue to put in place?

In addition, collaboration with medical professionals is essential to ensure the well-being of our clients. Imagine that a client has a toothache. Treating the toothache is not in the purview of a behavior analyst; however, teaching body part identification certainly might be, as well as teaching someone how to communicate when they are in pain—for example, once we have been able to identify that there is an "ouchie" in the mouth, we can work collaboratively with other medical professionals to alleviate the pain and address any challenging behaviors that may have been associated with pain attenuation. When we are unable to extend our competence quickly, or when someone else with expertise is available, we should be making appropriate client referrals. Our clients and their families have involved us in their care because they believe we can help. We are there to alleviate challenging situations, not make them worse. This means we must be sensitive to common stressors experienced by the families we serve, and we must actively seek to support the families in removing these stressors.

In Section 4, we dove into supervision requirements for behavior analysts and trainees that have been developed over time by the BACB, state licensure laws, and job-specific parameters. When we are providing supervisory services, as with anything else, we must continually improve our supervision skills. This means attending webinars, engaging with the literature, and employing the practices you learn. It is often suggested that supervisors and trainees develop an agenda for each meeting. Initially, the supervisor can take responsibility to develop the agenda and later transfer this responsibility to the trainee. The agenda may include terms to review and feedback from observations. We strongly suggest adding an intentional discussion pertaining to ethics in each session. Initially, you may need to provide some scenarios for your trainee; however, as unique situations arise frequently, it will not be long before your trainee is coming to you with scenarios and questions (e.g., inattentive supervisor, assigned to a new client with no training, uncomfortable statements by caregivers during the session, etc.). While there is no specific guidance on the number of trainees an analyst may supervise, it is wise to consider the (1) skill set of the analyst, (2) skill set of the trainee, (3) needs of each individual client, and (4) outcomes achieved.

Behavior analysts are responsible for the work conducted by the trainee and, therefore, must be diligent about not assigning tasks outside of one's scope of competence. While a supervisor may possess competence in a particular area—for example, treating severe problem behavior—they may not have experience working in a particular setting (e.g., public school), and while a supervisor may be a seasoned analyst, there are additional areas where they may not have any history or experience (e.g., consulting in a setting where you are an ethnic minority). It is for these reasons that we strongly encourage and support the recommendation that a trainee have multiple supervisors in the course of their preparation. When agreeing to take on a new trainee, we must recognize that we have the responsibility and expectation to use the science when teaching others about behavior analysis. This means providing immediate feedback, creating access to a dense amount of reinforcement, and following through on promises and agreements. By modeling the skills we want our trainees to learn and by discussing those skills with our trainees, we are likely to make a lasting impact on their practice.

In Section 5, we discussed the need to be truthful and accurate in the statements we make about behavior analysis. As analysts, we have the potential to help influence the conversation around the science and need to take care not to unintentionally overstate claims or exaggerate our outcomes. We want others to view us as reliable, dependable, and trustworthy. We are humans and we will make mistakes—that is not a problem. It would be a problem if we were to refuse to admit and learn from our mistakes. With regard to the statements we make, we must ensure that we are not providing treatment advice outside of a defined relationship, whether in person or online. Doing so could prove dangerous. There may be other medical or historical variables that have not been shared with us, or there may be an unhealthy or unsafe dynamic in the home to which we are not privy. Even in situations where direct harm may not occur, we are likely creating a situation that could delay the client or family from seeking ongoing support and consultation from an appropriate medical professional. Although well intended, our actions could have detrimental and negative consequences.

Behavior analysts historically have joined the field by way of various backgrounds, for example education, psychology, sociology, and speech and language pathology. Because of this, many of us possess dual skill sets, degrees, and certifications. The BACB recognizes this and supports the contributions of each credential. However, when we offer or make claims about behavior analytic treatments, we must do so in a way that accurately represents the field of behavior analysis. When we are providing access to information outside the scope of our BACB credential, we must ensure that we provide appropriate disclaimers to prevent any confusion from consumers.

Testimonials can be a compelling way to share feedback and garner supporters for a cause. Think about deciding where to go for dinner. Assuming you are new in town or want to try a restaurant that is new to you, what do you do? Most of us will look at images and reviews online. If a restaurant has delectable treats pictured that are accompanied by a one-star review, how likely are you to choose this restaurant over one that has a four- or five-star rating? The same is likely true for clients and families who are seeking services. They may want to see what other clients have said about the quality of the services. However, this is often difficult to do when it comes to the provision and delivery of ABA services. Historically, our Ethics Code has dissuaded us from soliciting, obtaining, or posting reviews from current clients but did leave room for testimonials from former clients. This latest iteration of our Ethics Code has seen an increase in the requirements that must be met in order to use testimonials. Testimonials from former clients must clearly indicate whether they are solicited or unsolicited, and we must review with the client how the testimonial may be used, the potential risks involved, and that they are aware they can rescind its use at any time. Solicited testimonials are not allowed from current clients, though there is recognition that current clients may freely choose to write an unsolicited testimonial on a website not controlled by the analyst (e.g., leaving a review on a web search platform). In such situations, analysts may not share or reuse that testimonial. Perhaps this will allow consumers more information moving forward when they are faced with identifying and selecting a high-quality agency and analyst with whom to work.

In the final section, Section 6, we discussed the need for research and the dilemmas that analysts can face when engaging in research. We looked at the disconnect between whether we should train practitioners to be researchers or to support researchers to better understand practice. This dilemma is not unique to behavior analysis. On average, the research-to-practice gap has been described as 17 years between the time a discovery is made and when it is implemented by practitioners—and that is across all sciences (Morris, Wooding, & Grant, 2011). When you are in the business of helping others and improving lives, shortening that gap is essential. It is vital to continue research to advance our field; however, that research cannot occur in a vacuum. When conducting research, we must take steps to protect our clients' well-being. Although we may be seeking answers to a particular question, when involving clients in research, we must ensure that the client benefits from participation. In order to appropriately recognize the contributions of the work being done, we also have an ethical obligation to provide proper credit to all contributors and co-authors. Failure to do so will have significant detrimental effects, including alienating research partners and colleagues by plagiarizing the work of others. Behaving in this manner could also call your research results into question. This can have a negative impact on you as a researcher-practitioner, as well as on the participants and the field as a whole.

Fortunately, systems are in place that help guide researchers through the process. Institutional Review Boards (IRBs) require us to produce (1) consent and assent for all participants, (2) a list of our contributors, and (3) the outline of the study and investigation, among other things. IRBs boards help us to ensure we are selecting procedures that are helpful, not harmful, to participants. However, this may present a barrier for any analyst who wishes to contribute to the research literature base but is not affiliated with any university. The increase in independent IRBs may help more analysts access the tools they need to engage in research. The Association for the Accreditation of Human Research Protection Programs (AHRPP) lists accredited boards from universities, hospitals, government entities, and independent review agencies.

While we hope we are able to provide you with some helpful solutions and starting points for addressing ethical concerns, we know that we cannot possibly cover every situation or scenario. No ethics textbook can, as details are different and our world is ever changing. The current iteration of our Ethics Code for Behavior Analysts was released in 2020 and went into effect in 2022. During those 2 years, our world changed drastically. For one, the COVID-19 pandemic was only beginning in the spring of 2020. We, as a field, had to navigate through pausing services and obtaining quick approval of telehealth services, while balancing our clients' needs for services with their needs for safety from a potentially deadly disease —as well as our own safety.

In the United States, we have also been dealing with an increased awareness of police violence against black communities and people of color. Traditionally, many of us were taught that community helpers were safe, including firefighters, police officers, postal workers, teachers, and others. Many of us have been led to believe these members of our communities are people we can trust. However, that is simply not the case for everyone—or, if it once was, it is no longer the case. From 2020 to 2022, there has been a societal uprising relating to police brutality in the United States, particularly since the deaths of George Floyd, Breonna Taylor, and Trayvon Martin, although there are many more. Sadly, this reality must change the way we think about and provide services. Acknowledging, rather than ignoring, these disparities will allow us to better differentiate instruction for our clients. In multiple situations, stereotypic behaviors that individuals exhibit (e.g., flapping hands) have been perceived as aggressive or noncompliant by law enforcement and can result in harm to clients or their caregivers. One hypothesis for why police officers make this assumption is that flapping one's hands is also a common behavior that methamphetamine addicts display (Egeland, 2017). In one publicized case, police officers detained a 14-year-old autistic male who they believed to be using an inhalant drug. Officer Grossman of the Buckeye Police Department, who was trained in drug recognition, went on record as saying "I observed some object in his right hand that he hit against his left palm and then he'd immediately bring his hands up to his face. It appeared he was smelling something" (Egeland, 2017). As behavior analysts, we recognize these behaviors as self-stimulatory; however, others without training may misinterpret these behaviors as potentially dangerous. While we must continue to advocate for societal equity and change, we must also focus on creating conditions and designing interventions that will keep our clients safe, happy, and healthy. When we have clients who do not respond to commands such as "Stop" or "Don't move," imagine the danger they are in, particularly if they are people of color. While many individuals in the autistic community tell us that behaviors such as flapping hands are calming, exhibiting these behaviors at the wrong time or place could prove deadly.

In the United States, we also have been facing an increase in mass shootings in recent years, including in our schools. This must change the way we think of safety drills. It is no longer enough to have our clients practice fire and earthquake and tornado drills, for example, but now we must also practice intruder and active shooter drills. Thinking through the potential situations, practicing with our clients, and doing our best to prepare them in case of a variety of emergency situations have become more vital than ever. However, it is also challenging to prepare our clients for horrific, potentially unlikely situations, without placing them under unnecessary distress.

In addition to practicing safety skills in schools, we must think through safety drills in homes. The September 26th Project provides some helpful tips on practicing fire safety with individuals who have an intellectual impairment. This project was started in the aftermath of a tragic fire that occurred in 2020 during the COVID-19 pandemic. Feda Almaliti and Muhammed, her autistic son, lost their lives on the morning of September 26. While Feda, her sister, and her niece were able to exit the home, Muhammed was not. With Muhammed inside the burning home, Feda ran back inside. They both perished due to smoke inhalation, simply because she was unable to compel her 15-year old, severely autistic, physically large son to go down the stairs and out the front door. With so many other skills needed to navigate his daily life, little emphasis had been placed on planning for emergencies of this magnitude. Perhaps that is why they did not survive. Perhaps they wouldn't have survived even with proper training or a formalized plan (The September 26th Project, 2021). Unfortunately, we will never know. We can, however, learn from this loss and use it as a reminder, as a motivator, for evaluating our current treatment goals and prioritizing scenarios such as this for our clients and their families.

We must also recognize the danger associated with wandering and drowning. "Nearly half (49%) of all autistic children elope and thus become subject to unsupervised dangers" (Martin & Dillenburger, 2019, p. 356). A study published in the *American Journal of Public Health* by Guan and Li (2017), "Injury and Mortality in Individuals with Autism," found that children with autism are at a significantly increased risk of wandering and drowning. In an interview with Columbia University, Li stated, "Children with autism are 160 times as likely to die from drowning as the general pediatric population". Li recommends that children with autism receive swimming lessons as early as possible to help increase their safety. Safety skills are vital. As our clients have a right to effective treatment, we must ensure that the skills we teach impact their lives in immediate, long-lasting, and positive ways. It is imperative that when making treatment recommendations, we continue to advocate for services to occur without restrictions on location, skill domain, or length of service.

Throughout each encounter and experience, we encourage you to approach situations with as much curiosity and compassion as possible. We also encourage approaching situations with skepticism and a keen commitment to doing what is in the best interest of our clients and the communities we serve. No one has all the answers. We are all capable of making mistakes. We are also capable of learning and growing from the mistakes we make. Even the most righteous and diligent individuals will find themselves tangled in sticky situations, seeking clarity where there is confusion. We encourage you to seek out mentors, be willing to have uncomfortable conversations, and be a resource and ally for one another. Above all, we encourage you to continue to grow alongside us. In order to actualize the potential of the science of behavior analysis, we need innovative thinkers and a continual commitment to evolving and elevating. In the words of Albert Einstein, "We cannot solve our problems with the same thinking we used to create them."

References

Cooper, J. O., Heron, T. E., & Heward, W. L. (2020). *Applied behavior analysis*. Pearson.

Egeland, A. (2017, September 19). *Police video shows Buckeye officer detain autistic teen he thought was using drugs*. The Arizona Republic. https://www.azcentral.com/story/news/local/southwest-valley/2017/09/18/police-video-shows-buckeye-officer-detain-autistic-teen-he-thought-using-drugs/679282001.

Guan, J., & Li, G. (2017). Injury mortality in individuals with autism. *American Journal of Public Health, 107*(5), 791–793. https://doi.org/10.2105/ajph.2017.303696

Kelly, A. N. (2015, September). *Coming together, keeping together: Maintaining momentum as a community*. Hawaii Association for Behavior Analysis Annual Conference.

Mailman School of Public Health, Public Health Now. (2022). *Individuals with autism at substantially heightened risk for injury*. Columbia University. https://www.publichealth.columbia.edu/public-health-now/news/individuals-autism-substantially-heightened-risk-injury-death.

Martin, C., & Dillenburger, K. (2019). Behavioural water safety and autism: A systematic review of interventions. *Review Journal of Autism and Developmental Disorders, 6*, 356–366. https://doi.org/10.1007/s40489-019-00166-x

Morris, Z. S., Wooding, S., & Grant, J. (2011). The answer is 17 years, what is the question: Understanding time lags in translational research. *Journal of the Royal Society of Medicine, 104*(12), 510–520.

Rosenberg, N. E., & Schwartz, I. S. (2019). Guidance or compliance: What makes an ethical behavior analyst? *Behavior Analysis in Practice, 12*(2), 473–482. https://doi.org/10.1007/s40617-018-00287-5

The September 26th Project. (2021). *Never forgotten*. Author https://www.september26.org/feda-and-mu.

Cumulative References List

American Psychological Association (APA). (2020). *Publication manual of the American psychological association* (7th ed.). Author.

Association for the Accreditation of Human Research Protection Programs (AHRPP). Home page. https://www.aahrpp.org.

Association for Science in Autism Treatment. (2022, June 29). Home page. https://asatonline.org.

Bannerman, D. J., Sheldon, J. B., Sherman, J. A., & Harchik, A. E. (1990). Balancing the right to habilitation with the right to personal liberties: The rights of people with developmental disabilities to eat too many doughnuts and take a nap. *Journal of Applied Behavior Analysis, 23*(1), 79−89. https://doi.org/10.1901/jaba.1990.23-79.

Behavior Analyst Certification Board (BACB). (2014). *Professional and ethical compliance code for behavior analysts*. Littleton, CO: Author.

Behavior Analyst Certification Board (BACB). (2020). *Ethics code for behavior analysts*. https://bacb.com/wp-content/ethics-code-for-behavior-analysts.

Behavior Analyst Certification Board (BACB). (2021). *BCBA examination pass rates for verified course sequences: 2016−2020*. https://www.bacb.com/wp-content/uploads/2021/06/BCBA-Pass-Rates-Combined-211129.pdf.

Behavior Analyst Certification Board (BACB). (2021). *Continuity of services: Managing service interruptions, transitions, and discontinuations*. https://www.bacb.com/wp-content/uploads/2022/01/Continuity-of-Services-Toolkit-220613.pdf.

California Code. (2013). Health and safety code − HSC. Division 20. Miscellaneous health and safety provisions. Chapter 1.3. *Human Experimentation*. Justia Law https://law.justia.com/codes/california/2013/code-hsc/division-20/chapter-1.3.

Carr, J. E., Austin, J. L., Britton, L. N., Kellum, K. K., & Bailey, J. S. (1999). An assessment of social validity trends in applied behavior analysis. *Behavioral Interventions, 14*(4), 223−231. https://doi.org/10.1002/(sici)1099-078x(199910/12)14:4<223::aid-bin37>3.0.co;2-y. 4<223::aid-bin37>3.0.co;2-y.

Carr, J. E., & Briggs, A. M. (2010). Strategies for making regular contact with the scholarly literature. *Behavior Analysis in Practice, 3*(2), 13−18.

Conners, B., Johnson, A., Duarte, J., Murriky, R., & Marks, K. (2019). Future directions of training and fieldwork in diversity issues in applied behavior analysis. *Behavior Analysis in Practice, 12*(4), 767−776. https://doi.org/10.1007/s40617-019-00349-2.

Cox, D. J., Plavnick, J. B., & Brodhead, M. T. (2020). A proposed process for risk mitigation during the COVID-19 pandemic. *Behavior Analysis in Practice, 13*(2), 299−305. https://doi.org/10.1007/s40617-020-00430-1.

Cox, D. J., Syed, N., Brodhead, M. T., & Quigley, S. P. (2022). *Research ethics in behavior analysis: From laboratory to clinic and classroom*. Elsevier Academic Press.

Critchfield, T. S. (2015). What counts as high-quality practitioner training in applied behavior analysis? *Behavior Analysis in Practice, 8*(1), 3−6. https://doi.org/10.1007/s40617-015-0049-0.

Daniels, A. C. (2009). *Oops! 13 management practices that waste time and money (and what to do instead)*. Performance Management Publications.

Department of Health and Human Services (HHS) Office for Human Research Protection. (2021, December 15). Subpart D - additional protections for children involved. https://www.hhs.gov/ohrp/regulations-and-policy/regulations/45-cfr-46/common-rule-subpart-d/index.html.

Doran, G. T. (1981). There's a SMART way to write management's goals and objectives. *Journal of Management Review, 70*, 35–36.

Egeland, A. (2017, September 19). Police video shows Buckeye officer detain autistic teen he thought was using drugs. *Arizona Republic.* https://www.azcentral.com/story/news/local/southwest-valley/2017/09/18/police-video-shows-buckeye-officer-detain-autistic-teen-he-thought-using-drugs/679282001.

El Fattal, R. (2022, May 23). *Robbie El fattal with Jonathan Tarbox and Amy Odum. YouTube. Other, Maraca Learning.* Retrieved May 24, 2022, from https://www.youtube.com/watch?v=0J8iRwlr-H0&t=2019s.

Fong, E. H., Catagnus, R. M., Brodhead, M. T., Quigley, S., & Field, S. (2016). Developing the cultural awareness skills of behavior analysts. *Behavior Analysis in Practice, 9*(1), 84–94. https://doi.org/10.1007/s40617-016-0111-6.

Foxx, R. M. (1996). Translating the covenant: The behavior analyst as ambassador and translator. *The Behavior Analyst, 19*(2), 147–161. https://doi.org/10.1007/bf03393162.

Freeman, T., LeBlanc, L., & Martinez-Diaz, J. (2020). Ethical and professional responsibilities of applied behavior analysts. In J. Cooper, T. Heron, & W. Heward (Eds.), *Applied behavior analysis* (3rd ed., pp. 757–782). essay, Pearson Education.

Guan, J., & Li, G. (2017). Injury mortality in individuals with autism. *American Journal of Public Health, 107*(5), 791–793. https://doi.org/10.2105/ajph.2017.303696.

Hanley, G. (2021, October 19). *A perspective on today's ABA from Dr. Hanley. Practical Functional Assessment.* Retrieved June 9, 2022, from https://practicalfunctionalassessment.com/2021/09/09/a-perspective-on-todays-aba-by-dr-greg-hanley/.

Holmes, O. W., & Novick, S. M. (1991). *The common law.* Dover Publications.

Johnston, J. M., Carr, J. E., & Mellichamp, F. H. (2017). A history of the professional credentialing of applied behavior analysts. *The Behavior Analyst, 40*(2), 523–538. https://doi.org/10.1007/s40614-017-0106-9.

Kelly, A. N. (2015, September). Coming together, keeping together: Maintaining momentum as a community. *Hawaii Association for Behavior Analysis Annual Conference.*

Kelly, A. N. (2018). Jennifer Lonardo on advocating for appropriate treatment recommendations (audio podcast episode). *Behaviorbabe.* https://anchor.fm/behaviorbabe/episodes/Jennifer-Lonardo-on-Advocating-For-Appropriate-Treatment-Recommendations-e2qj8p.

Kelly, A. N. (2018, April). *When professionals disagree: The ethics of effective collaboration.* Buellton; California: West Coast Conference on Autism. http://www.behavior.org/resources/1034.pdf.

Kelly, A. N. (2019a). Becky Markovits on making the most of online instruction (audio podcast episode). *Behaviorbabe.* https://anchor.fm/behaviorbabe/episodes/Dr–Becky-Markovits-on-Making-the-Most-of-Online-Instruction-e32fca.

Kelly, A. N. (2019b). E. Scott Geller on actively caring (audio podcast episode). *Behaviorbabe.* Retrieved March 7, 2022, from https://anchor.fm/behaviorbabe/episodes/Dr–E–Scott-Geller-on-Actively-Caring-e9tp32.

Kelly, A. N. (2019c). Elisa Cruz-Torres on RBTs: Ethics and advice (audio podcast episode). *Behaviorbabe.* https://anchor.fm/behaviorbabe/episodes/Dr–Elisa-Cruz-Torres-on-RBTs-Ethics-and-Advice-e35653.

Kelly, A. N. (2019d). Ellie Kazemi on the function of supervision (audio podcast episode). *Behaviorbabe.* https://anchor.fm/behaviorbabe/episodes/Dr–Ellie-Kazemi-on-the-Function-of-Supervision-e4t9be.

Kelly, A. N. (2019e). Kate Disney on accessing ABA for military families (audio podcast episode). *Behaviorbabe..* https://anchor.fm/behaviorbabe/episodes/Kate-Disney-on-Accessing-ABA-for-Military-Families-e3h7u8.

Kelly, A. N. (2019f). Lorri Unumb on autism insurance and adult services (audio podcast episode). *Behaviorbabe*. https://anchor.fm/behaviorbabe/episodes/Lorri-Unumb-on-Autism-Insurance-and-Adult-Services-e3a3et.

Kelly, A. N. (2019g). Rachel Taylor on defining the magic (Audio podcast episode). *Behaviorbabe*. https://anchor.fm/behaviorbabe/episodes/Dr−Rachel-Taylor-on-Defining-the-Magic-e3l4r8.

Kelly, A. N. (2019h). Tyra Sellers on supervision & stopping to smell the roses (Audio podcast episode). *Behaviorbabe*. https://anchor.fm/behaviorbabe/episodes/Dr−Tyra-Sellers-on-Supervision−Stopping-to-Smell-the-Roses-e4m6h4.

Kelly, A. N. (2020a). Antonio Harrison on turning on the lights (Audio podcast episode). *Behaviorbabe*. https://anchor.fm/behaviorbabe/episodes/Dr−Antonio-Harrison-on-Turning-On-the-Lights-e4o24p.

Kelly, A. N. (2020b). Jackie MacDonald on life-work balance (Audio podcast episode). *Behaviorbabe*. https://anchor.fm/behaviorbabe/episodes/Dr−Jackie-MacDonald-on-Life-Work-Balance-eahu3s.

Kelly, A. N. (2020c). Julia Fiebig on being okay with being uncomfortable (Audio podcast episode). *Behaviorbabe*. https://anchor.fm/behaviorbabe/episodes/Dr−Julia-Fiebig-on-Being-Okay-with-Being-Uncomfortable-e9ojci.

Kelly, A. N. (2020d). Justin Leaf on ensuring a bright future for our field (Audio podcast episode). *Behaviorbabe*. https://anchor.fm/behaviorbabe/episodes/Dr−Justin-Leaf-on-Ensuring-a-Bright-Future-for-Our-Field-ea456i.

Kelly, A. N. (2020e). Patricia Wright on cultural humility (Audio podcast episode). *Behaviorbabe*. https://anchor.fm/behaviorbabe/episodes/Dr−Patricia-Wright-on-Cultural-Humility-egq034.

Kelly, A. N. (2020f). Rose Griffin on being an SLP & BCBA (Audio podcast episode). *Behaviorbabe*. https://anchor.fm/behaviorbabe/episodes/Rose-Griffin-on-Being-an-SLP−BCBA-e4chbaKelly.

Kelly, A. N. (2021). Eileen Lamb on cyberbullying in the autism community (Audio podcast episode). *Behaviorbabe*. https://anchor.fm/behaviorbabe/episodes/Eileen-Lamb-on-The-Autism-Cafe-e11363.

Kelly, M. P., Martin, N., Dillenburger, K., Kelly, A. N., & Miller, M. M. (2018). Spreading the news: History, successes, challenges and the ethics of effective dissemination. *Behavior Analysis in Practice, 12*(2), 440−451. https://doi.org/10.1007/s40617-018-0238-8.

LeBlanc, L., Gravina, N., & Carr, J. E. (2011). Training issues unique to autism spectrum disorders. In J. L. Matson (Ed.), *Applied behavior analysis for children with autism spectrum disorders* (pp. 225−235). Springer. https://doi.org/10.1007/978-1-4419-0088-3_13.

LeBlanc, L. A., Nosik, M. R., & Petursdottir, A. (2018). Establishing consumer protections for research in human service agencies. *Behavior Analysis in Practice, 11*(4), 445−455. https://doi.org/10.1007/s40617-018-0206-3.

Mailman School of Public Health, Public Health Now. (2022). *Individuals with autism at substantially heightened risk for injury.* Columbia University. https://www.publichealth.columbia.edu/public-health-now/news/individuals-autism-substantially-heightened-risk-injury-death.

Malott, R. W. (1992). Should we train applied behavior analysts to be researchers? *Journal of Applied Behavior Analysis, 25*(1), 83−88. https://doi.org/10.1901/jaba.1992.25-83.

Martin, C., & Dillenburger, K. (2019). Behavioural water safety and autism: A systematic review of interventions. *Review Journal of Autism and Developmental Disorders, 6*, 356−366. https://doi.org/10.1007/s40489-019-00166-x.

McCullough, R. (2018). *Insider intelligence: Conflict in the workplace.* Security Info Watch. Retrieved July 20, 2022, from https://www.securityinfowatch.com/integrators/article/12399219/conflict-in-the-workplace.

Morris, Z. S., Wooding, S., & Grant, J. (2011). The answer is 17 years, what is the question: Understanding time lags in translational research. *Journal of the Royal Society of Medicine, 104*(12), 510−520.

National Autism Center at May Institute. National standards project. (2022). https://nationalautismcenter.org/national-standards-project.

National Standards Project. National Autism Center at May Institute. (2020). https://nationalautismcenter.org/national-standards-project.

Nochajski, S. M. (2002). Collaboration between team members in inclusive educational settings. *Occupational Therapy in Health Care, 15*(3−4), 101−112. https://doi.org/10.1080/j003v15n03_06.

O'Leary, P. N., Miller, M. M., Olive, M. L., & Kelly, A. N. (2015). Blurred lines: Ethical implications of social media for behavior analysts. *Behavior Analysis in Practice, 10*(1), 45−51. https://doi.org/10.1007/s40617-014-00330.

Phu, W., & Byrne, T. (2018). Testimonials on the web: Evidence for violations of the professional and ethical compliance code for behavior analysts. *Behavior Analysis: Research and Practice, 18*(4), 419−424. https://doi.org/10.1037/bar0000135.

Pokorski, E. A., & Barton, E. E. (2020). A systematic review of the ethics of punishment-based procedures for young children with disabilities. *Remedial and Special Education, 42*(4), 262−275. https://doi.org/10.1177/0741932520918859.

Purdue Writing Lab. (n.d.). Plagiarism overview. https://owl.purdue.edu/owl/avoiding_plagiarism/index.html.

Reid, D. H. (1992). The need to train more behavior analysts to be better applied researchers. *Journal of Applied Behavior Analysis, 25*(1), 97−99. https://doi.org/10.1901/jaba.1992.25-97.

Rosenberg, N. E., & Schwartz, I. S. (2019). Guidance or compliance: What makes an ethical behavior analyst? *Behavior Analysis in Practice, 12*(2), 473−482. https://doi.org/10.1007/s40617-018-00287-5.

Sellers, T. P., Valentino, A. L., Landon, T. J., & Aiello, S. (2019). Board certified behavior analysts' supervisory practices of trainees: Survey results and recommendations. *Behavior Analysis in Practice, 12*(3), 536−546. https://doi.org/10.1007/s40617-019-00367-0.

Shepley, C., Allday, R. A., & Shepley, S. B. (2017). Towards a meaningful analysis of behavior analyst preparation programs. *Behavior Analysis in Practice, 11*(1), 39−45. https://doi.org/10.1007/s40617-017-0193-9.

Skinner, B. F. (1953). *Science and human behavior.* Free Press.

Stone, D., Patton, B., & Heen, S. (2011). Difficult conversations: How to discuss what matters most. *Portfolio/Penguin.*

Taylor, B. A., LeBlanc, L. A., & Nosik, M. R. (2018). Compassionate care in behavior analytic treatment: Can outcomes be enhanced by attending to relationships with caregivers? *Behavior Analysis in Practice, 12*(3), 654−666. https://doi.org/10.1007/s40617-018-00289-3.

The Law Dictionary. (n.d.). Definition of intellectual property. https://dictionary.thelaw.com/intellectual-property.

The Law Dictionary. (2021, January 5). *What are some consequences of plagiarism?* https://thelawdictionary.org/article/what-are-some-consequences-of-plagiarism.

Tovino, S. A. (2020). Mobile research applications and state research laws. *Journal of Law Medicine & Ethics, 48*(S1), 82−86. https://doi.org/10.1177/1073110520917032.

U.S. Copyright Office, U. S. C. (n.d.). Copyright in general. https://www.copyright.gov/help/faq/faq-general.html#:~:text=When%20is%20my%20work%20protected,of%20a%20machine%20or%20device.

Van Houten, R., Axelrod, S., Bailey, J. S., Favell, J. E., Foxx, R. M., Iwata, B. A., et al. (1988). The right to effective behavioral treatment. *Journal of Applied Behavior Analysis, 21*(4), 381−384. https://doi.org/10.1901/jaba.1988.21-381.

Witts, B. N., Brodhead, M. T., Adlington, L. C., & Barron, D. K. (2020). Behavior analysts accept gifts during practice: So now what? *Behavior Analysis: Research and Practice, 20*(3), 196−202. https://doi.org/10.1037/bar0000117.

Wolf, M. M. (1978). Social validity: The case for subjective measurement or how applied behavior analysis is finding its heart. *Journal of Applied Behavior Analysis, 11*(2), 203−214. https://doi.org/10.1901/jaba.1978.11-203.

Wright, P. I. (2019). Cultural humility in the practice of applied behavior analysis. *Behavior Analysis in Practice, 12*(4), 805−809. https://doi.org/10.1007/s40617-019-00343-8.

Appendix B

Scenarios

Scenario 1:

You are consulting for a classroom in a local school district. When you are there to provide support for your client, the teacher tells you on your way out the door that the principal would like to talk to you about another student. When you stop by the principal's office, she asks that you stop in a neighboring classroom when you are on campus tomorrow and provide some strategies for a student in that room. You tell the principal you would be happy to assist, as long as you have consent from the family to collaborate on this child's team. The principal assures you they will get consent when they meet with the caregivers next. She reiterates the severity of the behavior and asks that you stop in tomorrow to see if there are any recommendations you can provide in the interim to the teacher for this student.

Scenario 2:

You are working for an ABA agency, where clients are assigned to you as availability opens on your schedule. Let's say you are one year postcertification, working for an agency that assigns you an 18-year-old client who has a diagnosis of oppositional defiant disorder (ODD). While obtaining your supervised fieldwork experience and in your first year as an analyst, you have only worked with clients ages two to six who have a diagnosis on the autism spectrum. You feel woefully unprepared and are extremely anxious about taking on this new client. What should you do? Use the six-step decision-making process to outline your options and determine the best course of action. Take into consideration the need to balance your current skill set with your obligation for professional development and growth. What might be two or three acceptable outcomes in this scenario?

Scenario 3:

You are working in an in-home setting, and during every session your client's grand-mother offers you scones. You politely decline and continue with your session. The grandmother interrupts each session, asking numerous times if you are well fed and if she can prepare any food for you. What would you do?

Scenario 4:

You collaborate and work with several colleagues of varying backgrounds and histories. On a video call, others observe you being a bit abrupt with one team member. This team member happens to be the only one of a particular gender on the call. While you may be responding to the individual regardless of gender, we must still ask ourselves these questions: "How is this dynamic influencing our decision making?" "Would we behave this way toward another colleague who is behaving in the same way regardless of their gender, age, status within the company, and so on?" "What can we do to test and challenge these beliefs?" "What steps can we take to ensure we are operating with equitable compassion and curiosity toward all our colleagues—and clients?"

Scenario 5:

You are working as a behavior analyst for an ABA agency, and your spouse has recently announced they wish to file for divorce. This comes on the heels of the news that your elderly mother received a recent diagnosis of Alzheimer's. While your personal life may be understandably overwhelming, you feel like you are able to focus on your clients. Over time, caregivers begin commenting to your employer that you have missed several sessions, which has compromised the reauthorization of service hours for the most recent treatment for at least one of your clients. What should you do now, considering the impact of your actions on your clients? What can be done to prevent the impact on your clients? What creative ways can you conceptualize protecting your clients, while honoring your need to grieve and heal balanced with your need to maintain a healthy income to sustain your livelihood and to provide for your children?

Scenario 6:

You are a behavior analyst who works at an agency that provides ABA services to children. As part of your work responsibilities, you also supervise individuals pursuing certification. Your boss approaches you about taking on a new supervisee, who happens to be his wife. You are uncomfortable saying no, but you also worry this will negatively impact your performance evaluation at work. In this case, your boss's wife is your superior's spouse, your colleague, and now potentially your supervisee.

Scenario 7:

You are working an 8-hour day, which is split between two clients who receive their services in-home, across town from one another. Most days, you bring a bottle of water with you. However, today you forgot. You mention being thirsty in the presence of the caregiver, who offers you a fresh bottle of water. Could accepting the water be classified as accepting a gift? Will this behavior constitute a multiple relationship? Will drinking the water present a conflict of interest?

Scenario 8:

You are working an 8-hour day that is split between two clients who receive their services in-home, across town from one another. You mention being tired in the presence of the caregiver, who offers you coffee. You hesitate but then decide that accepting the coffee is less problematic than falling asleep during your session. At your next session, the caregiver has a cup of coffee poured for you. However, today you had time to stop between sessions, and you brought your own coffee. The caregiver seems a little annoyed, commenting that they had bought the flavored creamer you had said you like. You offer your thanks for the coffee and say that there is no need to provide coffee for you in the future. The caregiver approaches the table where you are sitting with the client, picks up the cup of coffee, and pours it down the drain while exhaling an exasperated sigh.

Scenario 9:

You are working as an assistant behavior analyst for a relatively small organization. About a year into working for this organization, you have the opportunity to work one on one with a client in a public-school setting. You want to take the position; however, it is a bit farther away from the clinic, and with the increased cost associated with mileage it is not feasible for you to accept the position. The father of the client learns of this and wants to help. He asks what part of the town you live in and if there is anything he can do. You thank him for his interest, tell him where your apartment complex is, and assure him you will try to work something out. A few weeks later, on a Friday, you get a letter from the manager of your rental company saying that they are lowering your rent by $200 a month. There is no reason provided. You ask your neighbors if they received a similar letter. They received a letter, notifying them of a rental increase of $100 starting next month. They are upset with you for what feels like preferential treatment. You think about looking more into it, but then shrug it off. A few days later, you tell your agency you will take the position. On your first day at dropoff, the father makes a comment saying he is happy you took the job after all. He mentions talking to the manager of your rental property, saying something about being former college buddies. You realize the father "pulled some strings" so you could work with his child. In response to his comments, you smile and walk with your client into the classroom.

Scenario 10:

A client is receiving 20 hours a week of ABA services. The medical recommendation is for services to occur across settings, but the family is only interested in having in-home sessions, 4 hours a day. Due to staffing limitations and parental preference, only one technician is available to provide all 20 hours of care each week. There is no plan for adding an additional technician. What is the potential for harm?

Scenario 11:

You are working as a supervisor for a client receiving in-home services. You occasionally flirt with the neighbor, who eventually asks you out on a date. You check in with yourself and decide it is not a problem because the neighbor is neither the client nor a family member of the client. You go on a few dates, then the neighbor stops calling. You feel embarrassed and avoid going to the client's house for supervision, worried you will run into the neighbor. Eventually you ask for the case to be reassigned to another analyst, but there is no one available to take over for a few weeks. Since you are not comfortable going to the house, the company places the client's services on hold until a new supervisor can begin.

Scenario 12:

You are a professor who teaches undergraduate and graduate classes. You realize you have an attraction to one of your students, and the feeling appears to be mutual. Your student tells you they are interested in you sexually. You tell your student you think they are cute, but you cannot date students, despite the attraction. Six months later, the student graduates, obtains certification as a behavior analyst, and moves out of state. Several years later, you run into your former student at a conference. You talk for hours and have several drinks before you both head back to your room, where you spend the night together.

Scenario 13:

Considering scenario 12, let us look forward a few months into the future. Two months after returning from your conference travels, your university is hiring for a director of online learning. One of the applications in the stack of résumés was submitted by your former student who you recently reconnected with at the conference hotel. Before moving forward with the interviews, what steps should you take?

Scenario 14:

You learn that the organization where you have been working has submitted fraudulent claims under your name to health plans. Essentially, your signature was forged, and the health plans wer charged for services you did not provide. In this case, your employer has engaged in egregious acts and has put you and your clients at risk. You have not committed any violations or broken any laws, per se, but an investigation would show your name on the fraudulent claims. What steps should you take? What is your obligation for reporting this to the BACB?

Scenario 15:

You are working with a 10-year-old client who likes to listen to a particular song on repeat. The song he most strongly prefers is from a children's show, geared toward toddlers and preschool-age children. This fact does not bother your client, but the caregiver has mentioned that it is embarrassing to your client's brother, especially when he has friends at the house. The caregiver shared with you that one of the friends asked "Why does your brother listen to this music? Why does he listen to something so babyish?" The caregiver shared that the child was not trying to be rude or offputting but appeared sincerely inquisitive and seemed curious as to why his friend's older brother would enjoy music geared toward younger children. As an analyst, how would you respond to the caregiver?

Scenario 16:

You are working as an analyst for a company that determines which clients to assign to you. Your agency informs you of a new client whose needs you feel are outside your scope of competence. You push back and let your supervisor know of your discomfort. In response, your supervisor tells you that you are the only analyst who has availability to take on this client. If you are unable to add this client to your caseload, your supervisor tells you the client will be unable to access care. What should you do? Use the three questions posed by Rosenberg & Schwartz (2019) to guide your answer.

Scenario 17:

You send an email that includes some sensitive information to your supervisor about a shared client. However, instead of sending the email to your supervisor, you accidentally send the email to a professor who has the same name. You have accidentally shared confidential and sensitive client data with an unintended recipient. What steps do you take to immediately minimize and mitigate the risk of harm to your client?

Scenario 18:

You have been working with a client for 3 years at your current agency. Legally, you realize you must store records and maintain them for a period of 7 years. Two years after you and your organization discharge the client from care, you leave your current agency. You take a copy of the client records with you in case the funding source makes a request for information. Which ethical code elements have you violated? What is the risk of harm to the client? What should you do instead to protect yourself, your former client, and the organization?

Scenario 19:

You are working with a 25-year-old adult, who has a diagnosis of ADHD and health plan approval to receive behavior analytic services. The client wants to learn how to swim, and you agree that you can dedicate a portion of the session to teaching this skill. While learning to swim is an important life skill, you realize you do not have any goals in your treatment plan that are appropriate to teach at a community pool. In your session note, instead of listing the community as the location, you list the client's home. After all, you *did* start the session in the client's home. Is this decision ethical? Is it legal? What is the potential of harm to the client? What is the right thing to do?

Scenario 20:

You are providing support to a 9-year-old child and his family in their home. When conducting your interview, you ask about priorities for goals to address. The client and his mother provide you with a list of four behaviors they want to tackle with your support. The list includes learning to tie shoes, reducing aggressive behaviors, learning to ride a bike, and decreasing swearing behavior toward caregivers and younger siblings. How do you prioritize which behaviors to teach first? First, you are off to a great start by including the client as well as his mother in the discussion. Next, consider separating the client and his mother (e.g., one is on the couch in the living room and the other is at the kitchen table) and asking them to rank-order the four behavioral targets from most to least important.

Scenario 21:

You receive a request to consult with a 16-year-old and their caregivers. One of the behaviors of concern includes urinary accidents or "leaks." Before developing a behavior intervention plan, you recommend that the client receive clearance from a urologist. The family is a little bit hesitant; however, you remain firm and let them know you will develop an intervention once they receive clearance from a qualified physician. The family eventually schedules the appointment with the urologist. After the evaluation, the determination is made that the client has a defective bladder, which is contributing to the urinary accidents. Based on this information, you develop an intervention plan focusing on wearing, checking, and changing pantyliners and scheduling bathroom breaks, especially during highly preferred activities. How might you design the intervention plan differently without this medical consideration? Is it ethical to hold the client accountable for something that is not in their control? What might be the harm in doing so? This scenario is only an example that emphasizes the importance of seeking medical clearance, especially when treating complicated and complex behaviors.

Scenario 22:

You are conducting an initial assessment for a client who is 25 years old and described as being fully verbal. You have not worked with a client with this profile before. Typically, you work with early learners who are developing language, and for those clients you often select the Verbal Behavior Milestones Assessment and Placement Program (VB-MAPP), and generally you select the next three goals per domain in the same order as they appear on the assessment tool. You realize this assessment will not be acceptable for your incoming client, so you consult with your supervisor, who has more experience than you with older clients. She offers to train you in other assessments, such as the Essential for Living (EFL) and the Assessment of Functional Living Skills (AFLS), to co-conduct the assessment, and to assist with writing the treatment plan. Do these adjustments resolve all ethical concerns described in this scenario?

Scenario 23:

You are supervising a child's programming and see during a group circle time with others that the child repeatedly stands up during times when the rest of the group is sitting on the floor. The teacher gives the instruction to sit down, yet the child does not sit. You then direct the technician to remove the child from the activity. The child leaves while crying, hitting, and kicking. This behavior continues upon arrival in the session room, and the child starts to throw items from tables and cubbies. You direct the technician to remove the child from circle time in the future if not following instructions to sit with the group. What benefits does this intervention have? What risks does it have on the client? What can we do differently?

Scenario 24:

You work for an agency that uses an electronic data collection platform. When you start with the company, you are provided with training on the data collection system. When you go to input your programs, you notice the data collection tab defaults to displaying percentage data. You search until you find the appropriate dimension of measurement for the behavior of interest. You make a comment to your supervisor about how much effort it was to switch the dimension of measurement in the system, and you remark, "I wonder how many analysts end up selecting percent just because it's easier?" A few months later, a colleague transitions to a new position in the agency and you absorb some of that person's cases. When you do, you notice that for every behavior for each client, only percentage data are being collected, including when tracking tantrums and other behaviors, which are episodic in nature. You understand how this error happened but realize that the client's data displays are not painting an accurate picture. What would you do?

Scenario 25:

A child's grandparents contact you to start services for their grandchild. First, you may need to ask if they are custodial guardians for this child, or you may need to gather more information on the child's legal situation. If the grandparents are indeed custodial guardians, additional paperwork is necessary to demonstrate this legal relationship and ensure that you establish services with the stakeholder who has legal and medical decision-making rights for this child. If the grandparents are not the legal guardians but are helping the child's legal guardian by gathering information, you can tell them about your ABA services so that they can take the information back to the family. Could you directly contact the grandchild's legal guardian with only an inquiry from the grandparents? What ethical codes may impact this situation?

Scenario 26:

You have a client who turns 18 while actively receiving services with you. In the eyes of the government, the client becomes an adult. Caregivers may face difficult and lengthy paths in their state to establish guardianship if their child is unable to make medical and legal decisions for themselves. If the caregivers have legal guardianship, paperwork should be in the client's files. If caregivers have not yet obtained guardianship or do not need to do so, the client is now responsible for giving consent, in addition to assent for services received. Additional paperwork must now go directly to the client. The client will be responsible for signing any documents, such as treatment plans and consent for services. What should you do if the client does not want to continue services? What can we, as behavior analysts do, in situations such as these? We can explain the services that we have been providing and the current recommendation for services. We can advocate for continuing services until the client attains certain benchmark skills. Hopefully, we are involving our client in the decision-making process regarding treatment before they turn 18, and the client understands and agrees with the goals of treatment. Ultimately, the client in this situation has full power and rights to continue or stop services. We must support the client's rights even when we do not agree.

Scenario 27:

You are a brand-new, recently certified analyst. Your fieldwork and experience consist of children with autism, ages 2 to 7. You start at a new company and take over an existing caseload. While reviewing your clients, you see that one client is a 17-year-old who exhibits aggressive behaviors, including shoving, choking, hitting, punching, and kicking. Due to current staffing issues, the client is only receiving services for 10 out of 20 recommended hours. What is your ethical obligation regarding advocating for an appropriate service density? What steps should you take? How can you resolve this dilemma so that you follow the BACB Ethics Code, while allowing the client to receive effective services?

Scenario 28:

You work in a public school district. Your supervisor, the special education director for the district, contacts you by email requesting a functional behavior assessment (FBA) for a third-grade student. You respond via email that you can begin immediately. You ask for a copy of the student's IEP and written consent from the caregivers. Your supervisor informs you that the IEP and consent forms will be forthcoming. You reply to your supervisor that you will get started as soon as you receive the consent. She replies, "FBAs do not require consent," and instructs you to start the assessment the following day. You may find yourself having to make a very uncomfortable choice. Do you upset your supervisor, or do you engage in a potential ethical violation?

Scenario 29:

You are working at an ABA clinic with young children. Many of your clients also receive speech services, most from one company, although several high-quality speech practices are available. In the past, after making referrals to one agency, you received gift cards and bottles of wine for the referrals you made. Imagine you have a new client starting at your ABA organization and during assessment you determine that the client should also receive a screening for speech and language services. When providing the recommendation to the family, you provide only the name of that one company to the family. Which code elements apply to these ethical transgressions? What might you do instead?

Scenario 30:

Imagine a situation where a client is receiving 20 hours per week of direct therapy. Their technician quits suddenly and without notice. In this scenario, a large gap in the client's treatment sessions may result, or the client may find themselves in a situation where they are no longer receiving any services at all. As analysts, we must ensure that we have a general plan in place for these various types of situations to help minimize and mitigate the impact that a significant disruption, interruption, or delay can have on a client's outcomes (BACB, 2020 3.14). How could an analyst plan to minimize disruptions for a client receiving 20 hours per week? One idea may be to have multiple technicians working with the client. This way, if one technician leaves, the client will still be receiving a portion of their hours from other technicians on their team.

Scenario 31:

One of your clients receives 30 hours per week of services at the clinic. Data show that the client exhibits increased challenging behavior when unexpected disruptions occur (e.g., a technician cancels the session by calling out at the last minute). Early one morning, one of the technicians who works with the client for 3 hours during a midday session calls into the office and states they are sick and cannot make it to the session. What might the analyst do to avoid this disruption to the client's services?

Scenario 32:

A new client is starting services. During the assessment process, the analyst reviews how the home environment must be set up for services to take place in the home, including having a clean, separate area for sessions. When the analyst conducts the assessment in the home, nothing seems awry. About two weeks later, the analyst and technician arrive at the client's home for the first day of services. Upon entering the home, they notice that there is trash strewn across the floor and a strong, overpowering odor of stale cigarette smoke. What steps must the analyst take to address this concern? What would you do if the situation does not improve in a reasonable amount of time?

Scenario 33:

During the COVID-19 pandemic, many funders updated their policies surrounding supervision to allow for more telehealth delivery. While this helped increase the services that were provided during the pandemic, behavior analysts must always examine the decision to provide telehealth supervision from an ethical standpoint. Is this medically recommended for the client? Does it meet the funder's requirements? Does it meet the analyst's organizational requirements? What if it was a brand-new employee starting with a client? A behavior analyst must examine each individual situation and make the best choice.

Scenario 34:

A client with 20 hours per week has two technicians who each work 10 hours per week. Can an analyst supervise both technicians during the week? Most likely. What about a client with 20 hours per week who has 10 technicians each working 2 hours with the client? Can an analyst provide sufficient supervision of those technicians during the week? Most likely not. This would probably be a challenging endeavor even for a seasoned analyst, unless this was their only client.

Scenario 35:

Imagine that you are an analyst who has spent your career working in school settings. You are approached by a trainee who is working in a clinic and seeking a supervision contract with you. Although the trainee does have a supervisor for their direct services work in the clinic, that supervisor is unable to provide fieldwork supervision and no one else in the trainee's organization is available to provide mentoring in accordance with BACB standards. How would you handle this situation as the analyst? What considerations would you make? What protections would you want to put into place if you decided to take on the supervisee?

Scenario 36:

Imagine you have a 12-year-old client who receives services in the home. A few times a week, the client engages in aggressive behaviors, which include hitting and pushing others. The former technician who had been working with the client for 6 months recently resigned, and now a new technician is assigned to the case. Consider that the technician is new to the field, has successfully passed the competency assessment, and recently passed the test to become an RBT. Your schedule is packed full, with little flexibility for additional supervision, and you were not anticipating a new team member joining this client's team. You instruct the RBT to review the programs and behavior plan ahead of time, and you inform the RBT that you will check in after the session. Later that afternoon, the RBT calls the office to say they did not know what to do when the client tried walking away from the session, so they grabbed the client, which resulted in the client punching them in the face. What should the analyst do now? If we could turn back time, what might the analyst have done when a new team member was assigned to this case? What ethical codes may have been violated?

Scenario 37:

An analyst was recently asked to provide consultation with a client's family about toilet training. This client's funding source allows this service to be billed by an individual who is pursuing certification and accruing fieldwork hours. The analyst, being very busy, tells the trainee to conduct the training. In this scenario, the family will get the training they want without waiting for availability in the analyst's schedule, and the service provided is billable. Due to the analyst's hectic schedule, the trainee's materials are not reviewed ahead of time. What is the potential for harm to the client? What does it mean to be a good behavior analyst? What is the right thing to do?

Scenario 38:

A behavior analyst provides support and oversees services, which occur both in clinic and in homes. The analyst has a caseload of 10 clients with autism and a team of six behavior technicians. The employer requires all session notes, including supervision notes, to be completed at the end of each day. The analyst does not complete supervision notes one day. No one notices. A second day goes by. A third day goes by. Two weeks go by. The employer then notices that paperwork has not been completed. What are the ethical implications? What potential impact could this have on both the analyst and the technicians? What are the implications for the organization?

Scenario 39:

You are an analyst working in a school and providing supervision to behavior technicians who work directly with students. As part of your supervisory practices, you review and teach evidence-based practices. You have documented the supervision sessions and training topics. You overhear the technician telling a teacher you taught them that social stories are evidence based when you did not. What steps would you take next to correct this inaccuracy?

Scenario 40:

A company organizes training for all analysts and trainees, which includes topics on gender expression and identity. The presenter speaks about offering one's own pronouns to show acceptance of others and describes the difference in asking or stating someone's pronouns versus the person's *preferred* pronouns, with the perspective that accepting others is accepting that a person's pronouns are their pronouns and there are no such things as "preferred pronouns." Later, you are meeting with a trainee and discussing the training. The trainee knows someone who uses they/them pronouns but shares planning to refer to that individual as "she" because the persons "looks like a female." What might you do in this situation?

Scenario 41:

You are providing supervision in a group home and notice your team member does not have their tablet with them, which is how they record data. You remember that you have provided feedback in the past about this to the team member and also have it documented. This is impacting the client's progress, as there are not enough data to change targets. How would you address this occurrence with the employee? On top of the feedback provided today, your company's policies require a SMART goal since this same feedback has been given three times already. What SMART goal would you develop, and what are the next steps you will take?

Scenario 42:

You are an analyst in a school and are providing fieldwork supervision to a paraprofessional who also works in the school. You have been meeting bi-weekly at school with the trainee. It's now the beginning of May, and school will be out for the summer (3 months) beginning at the end of May. Your position does not require you to work through the summer. What must you do since you are supervising a trainee accruing fieldwork hours? What steps can you take to help your supervisee continue to obtain fieldwork hours if you are not available?

Scenario 43:

You are the only behavior analyst at a company's small, remote location. You have a team of four RBTs who you supervise. You have also been providing fieldwork supervision to one of the RBTs. A new opportunity has presented itself to you, and you have decided to move to a new state in 2 months for a new job. What are your obligations to the RBTs you are supervising? What would you do for the RBT who is accruing fieldwork hours?

Scenario 44:

You are at the state capital testifying in support of the need for licensure in your state. Legislators have asked for tangible examples of harm being done by unlicensed professionals. You speak with your clients, who provide you copies of emails, announcements, and meeting notes that address the questions posed by the legislators. However, when you submit this information to the chair and vice chair, you realize you did not redact the documents, which are now public record. What violation has occurred? What can you do to right this wrong? What can you do in the future to avoid revealing confidential information about active clients in your public statements?

Scenario 45:

You are being interviewed on the news for your experience and expertise on treating individuals with ADHD. While being interviewed, you are asked to share a success story. You do, being careful not to mention names or the location where the individual lives. You also choose to share about a former client who no longer lives in the same region as you. In this situation, with the protections put into place, do you feel there is any potential of harm to the individual whose story you referenced? Would your answer be different if it were a current client?

Scenario 46:

You are reading posts online on social media, and you see a caregiver asking for help about teaching her child to use the bathroom independently. You know of some great strategies, so you comment in the thread on what she can do to help her child. What is the potential risk of harm for the child? The caregiver? What information could you have provided instead of ideas on specific strategies to try?

Scenario 47:

You attend a presentation sponsored by your local state chapter. At the conference, a presenter speaks on a topic that you are interested in learning more about. The presenter offers to share their slides after the conference with all attendees. Eager to disseminate this information to your colleagues, you use the speaker's slides to present at a monthly analyst meeting, which is recorded. While presenting, you mention that you received the slides directly from the presenter. However, you omit from the discussion the fact that you did not tell the speaker you would be presenting the slides and content verbatim. Consider what is problematic with this and identify different actions that could be taken.

Scenario 48:

You are employed by an agency that has solicited testimonials from current clients. Although your boss/employer is not a behavior analyst, you feel uncomfortable with how testimonials are being obtained and how they are being used to recruit new clients, particularly when current client schedules are not maximized. What should you do?

Scenario 49:

You are working with a client with limited verbal communication. You decide you want to do some research on which is the best method of communication for this client, as well as several others who are not developing vocal speech. You design a study, go through an IRB, have the appropriate consent, and are ready to begin. In this project, you are comparing sign language and Picture Exchange Communication System (PECS). However, this client begins to increase their vocalizations and engages in aggression when you try to prompt them to sign. They are now in the PECS phase; however, your study calls for a reversal where you are to reintroduce sign language with the client. You want to continue your study but are concerned with the increase in aggression. What do you do? Use the questions posed by Freeman, LeBlanc, and Martinez-Diaz: "What is the right thing to do? What is worth doing? and What does it mean to be a good behavior analyst?" (Cooper et al., 2020, p. 757).

Scenario 50:

You have finished your research study, using eight participants. You want to display their data and present your research at your local chapter's ABA conference. You have permission to present from all participants' guardians. You put your poster together using fake names for your clients; however, you include individual age, ethnicity, and gender for each client. Your employer asks that you put the company's name on your poster. You live in a small community and are afraid that some individuals at the conference may be able to figure out who the clients are based on your employer and the identifying information you have used. What are the problems associated with including the employer's name? What other steps could you take to ensure that you prevent the disclosure of confidential information?

Scenario 51:

You have been invited to participate in a publication on public policy and advocacy because your involvement in these activities is widely known and well respected. You agree to participate with two other individuals, one of whom is a student completing their doctorate program. You and this student work together closely on the project, and together you complete the lion's share of the work. The third author, who originally organized the partnership, has only been available to provide some opinions and light editing on the sections you and the student have written. When the project is complete and you are ready to submit the publication for consideration, you learn that you are listed as the third author. What potential violations have occurred? What can you do to address and resolve your concerns? What steps can you take in the future to avoid finding yourself in a similar predicament?

Index

Note: Page numbers followed by f indicate figures, t indicate tables, and b indicate boxes.